TEACHING PRIMARY SCIENCE

Seeds and seedlings

Dorothy Diamond

A Chelsea College Project sponsored by the Nuffield Foundation and the Social Science Research Council

Published for Chelsea College, University of London, by Macdonald Educational, London and Milwaukee

First published in Great Britain in 1975 by
Macdonald & Co (Publishers) Ltd
Maxwell House
74 Worship Street
London EC2A 2EN

Reprinted 1977, 1978, 1979, 1981, 1983

ISBN 0 356 05072 6

Library of Congress Catalog Card Number
77-82986

Printed in Great Britain by
Butler & Tanner Ltd, Frome and London

Project team

Project organizer: John Bird

Team members: Dorothy Diamond (full-time)
Keith Geary
Don Plimmer
Ed Catherall

Evaluators: Ted Johnstone
Tom Robertson

Editors

Penny Butler
Macdonald Educational

John Pettit
Nuffield Foundation Science Teaching Project
Publications Department

General preface

The books published under the series title Teaching Primary Science are the work of the College Curriculum Science Studies project. This project is sponsored jointly by the Nuffield Foundation and the Social Science Research Council. It aims to provide support and guidance to students who are about to teach science in primary schools.

Although the College Curriculum Science Studies materials have been produced with the student teacher very much in mind, we suggest that they will also be of use to teachers and to lecturers or advisers—in fact to anyone with an interest in primary school science. Hence this series of books.

Three main questions are considered important:

What is science?

Why teach science?

How does one teach science?

A very broad view is taken of teacher training. Training does not, and should not, stop once an in-service or college course has been completed, but can and does take place on a self-help basis in the classroom. In each context, however, we consider that it works best through the combined effects of:

1 **Science** Science activities studied practically at the teacher's level before use in class.

2 **Children** Observation of children's scientific activities and their responses to particular methods of teaching and class organization.

3 **Teachers** Consideration of the methods used by colleagues in the classroom.

4 **Resources** A study of materials useful in the teaching of science.

5 **Discussion and thought** A critical consideration of the *what*, the *why* and the *how* of science teaching, on the basis of these experiences.

To help with this choice there are, at frequent intervals, special points to consider; these are marked by a coloured tint. We hope that they will stimulate answers to such questions as 'How did this teacher approach a teaching problem? Did it work for him? Would it work for me? What have I done in a situation like that?' In this way the reader can look critically at his own experience and share it by discussion with colleagues.

This is particularly important because we feel that there is no one way of teaching, any more than there is any one totally satisfactory solution to a scientific problem. It is a question of the individual teacher having to make the 'best' choice available to him in a particular situation.

All our books reflect this five-fold pattern of experiences, although there are differences of emphasis. For example, some lay more stress on particular science topics and others on teaching methods.

In addition, there is a lecturers' guide *Students, teachers and science* which deals specifically with different methods and approaches suitable for the college or in-service course in primary science but, like the other books in the series, it should be of use to students and teachers as well as to lecturers.

Contents

Introduction

This is a traditional topic for school classrooms, but it may be looked at in many new ways and these can be made suitable for any age group from infant to university level.

The material is of vital interest to mankind for his survival, and it is easy for even the youngest pupil to become involved in growing things, one of man's oldest activities on earth.

Scientific attitudes can be built up from the very beginning, starting with observation. Classifying, experimenting, measuring and recording, the making and testing of hypotheses, controlling variables in experimental work—all these essentials of scientific thought and action can be introduced and practised during learning about seeds and seedlings.

Class and classroom organization

Among the special problems of this topic are:

The need for standing room for pots, etc.
The time factor.

A child's time is *now*, but seeds will not produce instant seedlings. What does one do, and more important, what do all the children do, between seedtime and harvest?

This book contains many suggestions for organization and for activities to help solve these problems. Some points occur more than once, but this is to make *choice* possible; lecturers, students in curriculum courses and teachers in classrooms may well wish to select material to fit their current needs.

Give children *some* help, but make sure they have part of each problem to solve for themselves.

Collect as many of their ideas and experiences as you can, for your own future use. Have up your sleeve your own solution to each problem.

'It is a good sign of learning when children say "Let's try it, let's plant it, let's grow it." They are evolving a belief in their own ability to answer questions.' (Elementary Science Study, *Teacher's Guide: Growing Seeds*)

See bibliography: 9, 10.

1 Starting and sorting

Students in colleges, students on teaching practice and teachers in service all tend to be heard saying 'We can't do this or that activity—there isn't any money.' It may not be an insoluble problem, but since this is the way they see it, cost must be considered.

Getting seeds

Some seeds will need to be bought, especially in towns. (Old packet seeds are often very disappointing; they may just be dead.) Value for money suggests mustard, cress, dried food peas and beans, orange and apple pips, maize, oats, wheat, sunflower and lawn grass seed.

Others can be found *wild*: sycamore, horse-chestnut (under the trees in late spring), acorns, dandelion or groundsel fluffy fruits, etc.

Note: some will only grow in spring (they survive by being dormant through the winter); some germinate very slowly. *Test first.*

Seeds can be obtained from the garden, or from a friendly farmer. Here are some suggestions:

Antirrhinums, poppies.
A last *dry* pod on a runner bean plant.
Lupin seeds from autumn pods.
Wheat, oats.
Grass.

Caution Laburnum seeds are poisonous.

Pips, seeds and 'stones' from the kitchen can also be used: for example, apple, orange, lemon or grapefruit pips. (These grow well, but not always quickly.)

Avocado stones may take months; date stones need warmth. Would rotten fruit be any use?

Note: some seeds will have been cooked or frozen. *Check the seeds' background (eg roasted peanuts).*

Getting containers

This is the least difficult. Plastic cream, yoghurt, margarine and icecream tubs can be had for the asking, as can used plastic beakers and all kinds of egg boxes.

How are these to be (a) cleaned if necessary, (b) stored until needed, (c) labelled when in use?

How will you and the children make the holes in the bottom for drainage?

What trays will you stand them on?

Getting material for seeds to grow on or in

Soil is free, but very messy, and variable. Sand brings similar problems. Cottonwool and blotting paper are traditional but expensive. *Vermiculite* is excellent (light, granular, clean and easily moistened) but expensive to buy. Sawdust is cheap, and very good.

Try a few school paper towels or a little toilet tissue (not the impervious paper).

The best idea of all is to find a shop, warehouse or workshop which has objects packed in Vermiculite to prevent breakage. As the Vermiculite is thrown away it will probably be available.

Get a few interested pupils to suggest sources of material; they often think or know much more about the resources of their environment than adults do.

What types of suggestion do you get from the children?

Classification: sorts of seeds

Collect small dishes of several different well-known kinds of seed. The larger seeds are best for ease of vision and handling.

Think of ten different ways to group these, without being academic. Perhaps you could try the following:

1 Wild/farm or garden.
2 Longer than 1 cm/shorter than 1 cm.
3 Food/not food (for people and animals).
4 From trees/not from trees, etc.

What do you sort seeds into? Specially bought sorting trays may be too expensive and make it into a 'lesson' only done in a classroom. Try to keep the idea that containers should be similar and standard by using any plastic icecream, yoghurt or margarine tubs you have.

Keeping to a standard set of equal containers gives a visible indication of comparative sizes; this is useful even if not exact. (See bibliography: 14.)

Bearing in mind the criteria you have chosen, talk with the children and get their ideas for groups. The more ideas you try, the more useful the exercise can become.

Perhaps the children have met Venn diagrams and intersections in their number work; if so, they might combine two ideas, say nos 2 and 3 above, but this should not be forced.

For example:

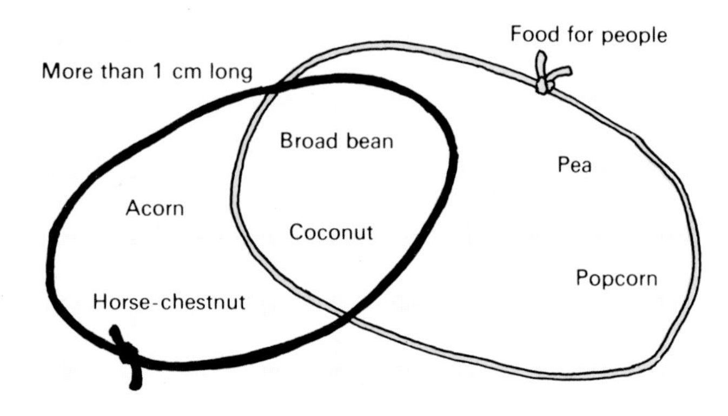

Now think about the odd ones out: the date stone which won't crack, or the strawberry pips on the outside of the strawberry.

As an adult, you see here the problem of any classification: do you lump things together or split them up? Dienes' logic blocks are man-made and easy to group; natural things are sometimes almost impossible to classify. In fact, dates are grouped with grapes (not plums), but whereas grapes may have several pips, dates only have one pip, the 'stone'.

Simple grouping or classification is a very early (natural or learnt) activity of children. What examples from everyday life can you suggest that might be used in discussion with children to give them some idea of the reasons for sorting (for example, supermarkets)?

A note about sorting

Alternative methods of sorting are:

1 The teacher does the sorting herself in front of the class, discussing with the children and getting their ideas at the same time.

2 One or more groups of children do the sorting themselves.

Each method has its advantages; the first perhaps making control and organization easier, the second allowing children to have more practical experience. Which would you choose? Why?

Here is a transcript of a tape-recorded conversation with children, aged six, sorting seeds:

Teacher: 'Now what about these things here, what else is there to look for?'
Samantha: 'They're nuts.'
Teacher: 'They're nuts? I see.'
Samantha: 'Mummy's growing vegetables.'
Teacher: 'So we've got all these things here.'
Samantha: 'They're pebbles.'
Teacher (pointing to the pebbles): 'Why do you say that they are pebbles, and these other things aren't?'
Samantha: 'They're big, and they're very smooth and round.'
Teacher: 'Yes, but these seeds here, they're smooth, and those bean things here are big and smooth. But what's the difference between those pebbles and the seeds?'
Samantha: 'Well, they're bigger.'
Teacher: 'I see. What about these things here?'
Samantha: 'They're sea stones.'
Teacher: 'Why didn't you say that these are stones—these seeds?'
Samantha: 'They rattle!'
Teacher: 'Which of these things grow, and which don't grow? Or do they all grow?'
Samantha: 'Those grow and those grow, and *those* grow and they grow. They don't grow; they don't.'
Teacher: 'Why?'

Samantha: 'They're solid hard and they won't crack.'
Teacher: 'Why is it that if they crack that would make them seeds? When you say cracked, do you mean split open?'
Samantha: 'The seeds crawl out of their things, don't they? You know. They move theirselves—they move their way out! The seeds.'
Teacher: 'What do you think, Simon?'
Samantha: 'That's what Daddy says.'

There are many types of criteria: those based on use, location, size and shape; subjective criteria such as 'I like this', and so on. Which types does Samantha use in this conversation?

What criteria do your pupils choose? How much do they differ from those which you had in mind?

The classification of living things

Here are some of the Science 5/13 Objectives for children learning science:

Ability to group things consistently according to chosen or given criteria.
Ability to make comparisons in terms of one property or variable [for example, shape, size or texture].
Interest in comparing and classifying living or non-living things.
Ability to group living and non-living things by observable attributes.
Ability to classify living things and non-living materials in different ways.

Look back at the conversation between the teacher and Samantha. So far as work with seeds is concerned, what evidence have you that any of the above Objectives have already been achieved by these children?

For example, are the criteria they have used held consistently?

What is a seed?

Helping children to develop their own ideas

Here is a transcript of a tape-recorded conversation with children, aged eight, who have already grown seedlings from seeds.

Teacher: 'Is a seed the only thing a plant can grow from? What do you think, Julia?'
Julia: 'Well, I don't really know any other things but I've a feeling that they can grow other ways.'
Teacher: 'Can you think of any other ways?
Paul: 'Yes, a bulb.'
Teacher: 'A bulb—is a bulb a seed?'
Paul: 'Yes, it's a kind of seed itself.'
Quentin: 'No, it can't be a seed.'
Teacher: 'Why do you say it's not a seed, Quentin?'
Quentin: 'Well, for a start, it's much much bigger.'
Teacher: 'Where do seeds come from then?'
Quentin: 'Well, the seeds come from a flower. There are lots of seeds in the centre of the flower and they just spread out.'
Teacher: 'OK. David said he thought a bulb was a seed.'
David: 'Well, it is. If a coconut's a seed, that's big, so a bulb must be a seed.'
Julia: 'Well, seeds tend to be much smaller. I don't know, I just think they are different.'

1 Collect actual examples or pictures of some seed-pods or other fruits, which have *obviously* come from flowers, for instance dandelion heads, antirrhinum pods, bean-pods with remains of flowers still attached. Observe the fruits and seeds. (Seeds are found inside seed-pods or other fruit.) These examples might help to support the arguments of the children who hold Quentin's view.

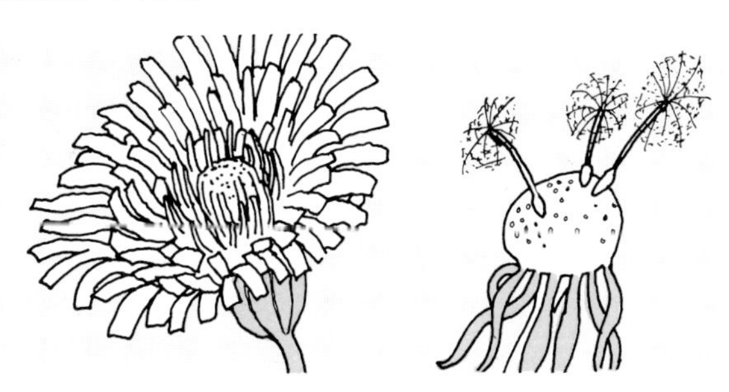

2 Find some bulbs showing green leaves from the *old* plant, with a new bulb or two at the base. These considered side by side with the fruits of no. 1, may make observations possible which would help Paul to go further. For example, some plants use two different ways of making more plants.

3 Display, side by side, onion bulbs and onion seeds, with the seed packet or a label for identification.

On what different criteria do David and Quentin base their idea of a seed? To what extent do you think the teacher is justified in guiding the discussion rather than straightforwardly telling the children the answer?

Can you find any way of dealing with the problem of the coconut as stated by David on page 5?

Another transcript Here is a discussion between the teacher and Colin and Diana (aged eight and ten).

Teacher: 'Now, would you like to tell me what you think a seed is?'
Colin: 'Well, it is something that comes from a plant.'
Teacher: 'Comes from a plant?'
Colin: 'Well, when you get a tree sometimes a seed blows off and falls onto the ground and then they start growing again.'
Teacher: 'Is anything that comes from a plant a seed?'
Colin: 'It grows.'
Teacher: 'Where do seeds actually come from?'
Colin: 'From flowers or something, something that passes it on.'
Teacher: What part of the plant?'
Colin: 'From the inside.'
Teacher: 'Do you know where in the inside?'
Colin: 'In the middle. If you have a rose, before it opens up, in the very middle, there is a little seed that is passed on.'
Teacher: 'What part of the plant does it come from?'
Colin: 'In the rose, does it come from the rose hip?'
Teacher: 'From the rose hip?'
Colin: 'Yes, it is sort of like a little red thing and when it drops on the floor . . . it's like a bud and I think it contains some seeds inside it.'
Teacher: 'What part of the plant do you think the seeds come from?'
Diana: 'Under the flowers is this seed box. When the plant dies the seeds ripen. It bursts open and the seeds fall out.'
Colin: 'And they go in the earth.'
Teacher: 'Where do seeds come from?'
Colin: 'The market.'

What experiences do you think these children need, to help clarify their ideas? Many children think that the market is the ultimate source of seeds. Was this Colin's idea or are there other possible explanations for children thinking this?

2 Sizes of seeds: measurement

Length and width

From cress to coconut, the sizes of seeds can be very interesting. Decide what *kind* of dimension to measure first; try it with a varied set of seeds.

Coconut-shaped objects are not easy to measure, but this method uses everyday apparatus (see also page 48)

When deciding what seeds to give children to work with, think first, and choose the seeds carefully.

Try several techniques for measuring length:

1 One seed (a bean?) on a ruler.

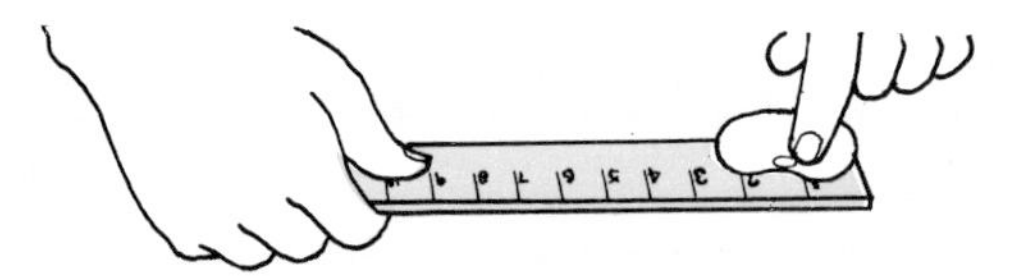

2 Seeds laid end to end along measured centimetres on paper (for example, cress). Then try side by side.

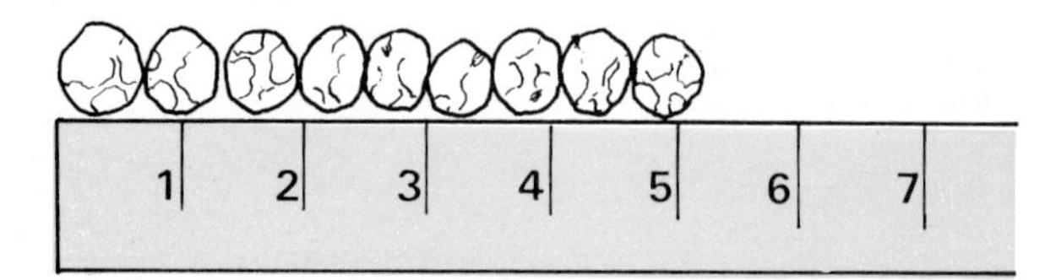

3 A simple caliper method.

Try measuring lengths and diameters of rounded objects such as conkers or cobnuts. Make your own sliding calipers. Juniors could also make these themselves. (How do they cut the two slits but nothing else?)

4 Measure the circumference of a seed. A large one, as in the picture below, will give the best results.

For a better estimate of size, two dimensions may be used. How many peas can you pack on to a 3-cm square (only one layer, of course)? What about widths? Some seeds are long but narrow, such as oats. Does this help towards a concept of average size? For example, how many oats can you pack on to a square of the same size?

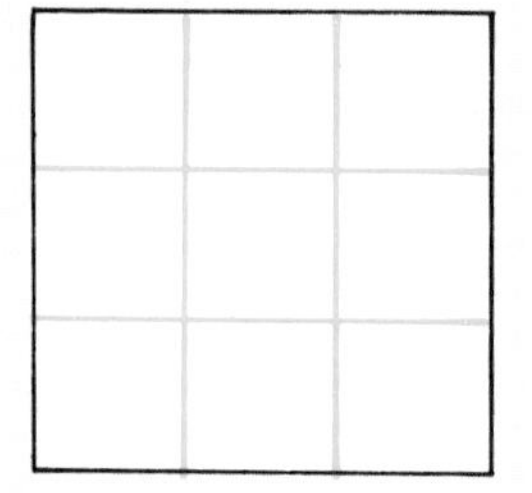

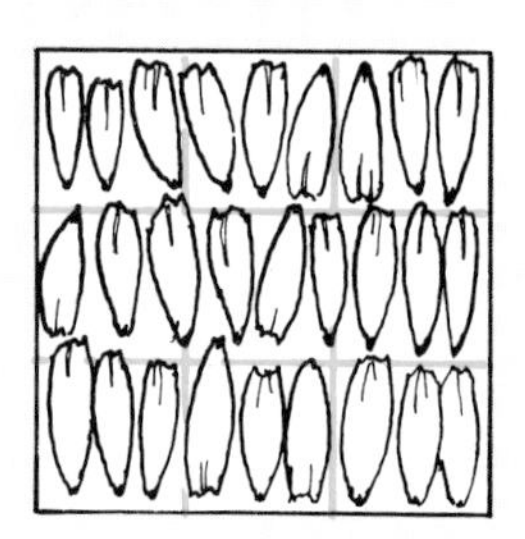

Would it be a good idea to duplicate squares (on paper or card) for class use? This depends on the class; some pupils might lose sight of the purpose of the square during the process of drawing it.

Volume

Crude volume (the space occupied) In terms of an arbitrary but familiar container, this may be the best starting point. How many dried peas, beans, mustard seeds, or conkers will go into an egg-cup? Should the objects in the container be smoothed off or heaped? This gives a view of scientific method, from more than one aspect.

Record the results and ideas from individuals and groups.

You can go on to use standard metric containers. A litre, a 10-cm cube, is a bit too big. Small plastic measuring jars are good for *small* seeds.

Stop for a moment to consider the two ends of the range: cress seeds (for most people these are too small to count) and a coconut (sit it on the egg-cup!).

Of course, seeds can be dropped into water to see how much the water level rises. This makes the seeds wet, and it is probably best tried just before they are to be grown. In any case, this method involves two intellectual steps, and needs experience (see Chapter 4).

Look for abilities and difficulties in measuring at different developmental stages.

What special problems do you find children experiencing with manipulation and with concepts of size?

Measurement of living things

Here are some Science 5/13 Objectives for children learning science:

Awareness of the meaning of words which describe various types of quantity.
Development of concepts of conservation of length and substance.
Appreciation of the need for measurement.
Development of concepts of conservation of weight, area and volume.
Ability to choose and use either arbitrary or standard units of measurement as appropriate.
Recognition of the need to standardize measurements.

Which of these objectives do you consider any of your pupils are capable of achieving?

3 Planting seeds

Children can often solve practical problems in their own ways, but make sure you have your own solution in reserve.

Make, and encourage children to make, notes, recordings, sketches, photographs, models, transparencies, etc, showing the original ideas, and then any successful results.

Containers Seed-growing experiments need pots, such as jam jars or yoghurt pots with holes in the bottom. Try for yourself first, but listen to children and decide together.

An egg box in a plastic bag, with lolly-stick supports, makes a mini-seedbed. Would you use an egg box of papier mâché or of plastic?

Labels Seed pots need labelling with the names of the seeds, the owners, or both, and also possibly with the date and/or special conditions. What would be good ways of doing this labelling? Think of several ways, and try the most feasible. What stands up best to water?

Soil The seeds need 'soil' of some sort (a medium). Why? What jobs has the soil to do?

Will you expect clay, sand, John Innes seed compost, cottonwool, paper towels or Vermiculite to be good? Try several. Which is best? Which will you recommend to children later?

Germination This process is more interesting if samples can be *watched* through all stages; however, this may need very artificial conditions, especially to make the roots visible throughout. Try the following constructions (and see bibliography: 21):

Seeds on blotting paper in a saucer (this dries up).
Traditional jam jar with rolled blotting paper lining. (This is not easy; the seeds tend to drop to the bottom.)
A sandwich made from glass, or glass and hardboard sheets, with seeds and a damp tissue, or a little damp cottonwool between.
Loose cottonwool in a vertically supported Petri dish, with Sellotape round the dish.

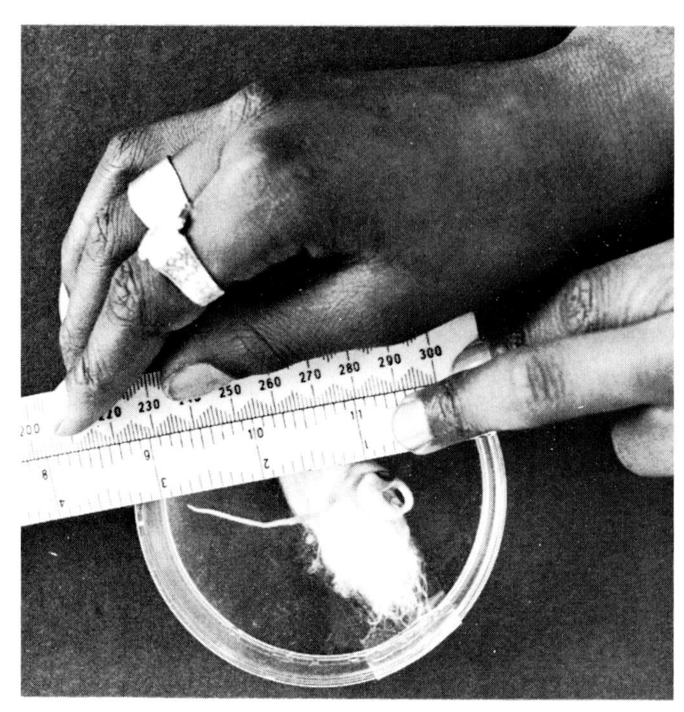

Watering Seeds and seedlings need watering in their pots. Try it in different ways. Will you use pure water or tap water? How much? From what?

Pots tend to dry out over the weekend; this may well be fatal to seedlings and experiments. How do you prevent this? Do you give extra water or put the pot and seedlings inside a plastic bag?

Can you think of other methods, such as:

Porous or perforated pots standing in trays of wet gravel?
Mini-greenhouses, with wire frames and large, clear plastic bags?

Standing room This is often very scarce in a classroom, especially if it is needed for weeks at a time. Let the children consider this; listen to their ideas. (They will probably see very early that the other main problems are leakage and breakage. Leaking water can easily spoil paint or varnish.)

What solutions can you and the children find? Consider:

1 A firm temporary shelf supported above a windowsill.
2 An orange box without top or bottom.
3 A tray slung below a shelf.

4 The bath sponge-tray.
5 A mini-greenhouse *outside* the window (see bibliography: 24, 25).

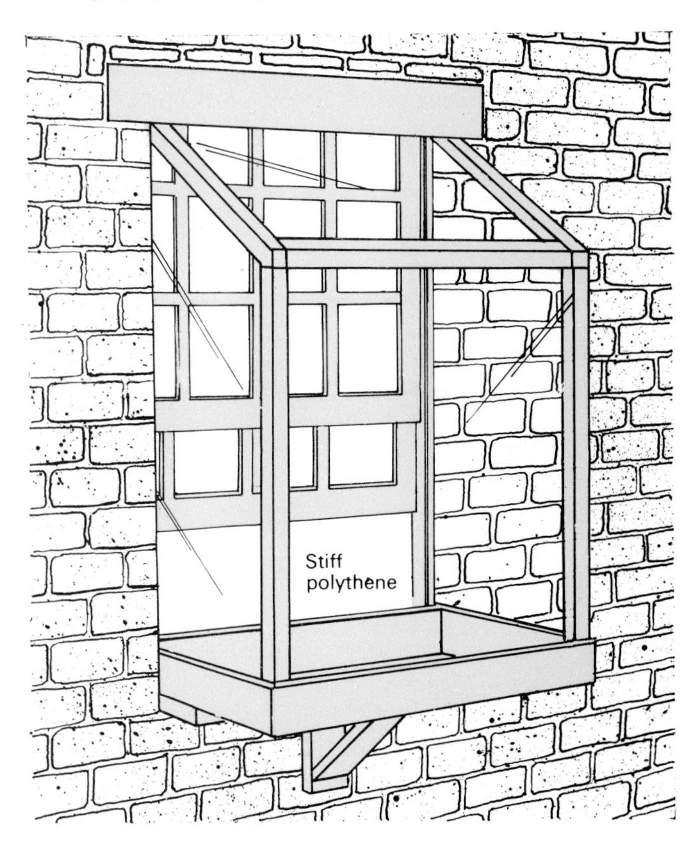

Darkness Some experiments may need pots to be kept in the dark, but cupboard space may be unsuitable or non-existent. What ways can you think of to keep the seeds or seedlings in the dark, while changing other conditions as little as possible?

Support Supporting seedlings, such as runner beans, can also be a problem. All classroom seedlings tend to be spindly, so help is essential, particularly if a complete life cycle is hoped for. Look at seed packets to find the expected height.

Would you try some methods without seedlings first, to avoid damage?

Could the seedlings be supported with sticks, wires, thin garden cane, cotton or string? Perhaps a box could be made with a trellis built on. (Fathers may well find this a challenge at the weekend!) The plastic bag is not needed after the seedling stage.

Discuss:

'Children need to be shown how to make apparatus.'
'Children learn best by inventing apparatus for themselves.'

How far would you steer children away from choices which are heading for failure?

4 Soaking seeds in water

Seeds in packets are always quite dry. Seeds bought as animal food (sunflowers, birdseed, oats for ponies, etc) also are always quite dry. What difference does soaking in water make?

Length and width

Using the techniques described in Chapter 2, measure with rulers, calipers and drawn squares the lengths and widths of some dried peas.

Then count the peas and soak them. After twenty-four hours drain and dab them dry, and again test against the original measures.

Volume

Measure out some dry peas with an egg-cup, small cream pot, or similar container filled till the seeds lie level with the top.

Older pupils may well see that the egg-cup measure does not accurately show the volume of the peas, since there are spaces between them.

Then soak these peas in a larger pot of water for about twenty-four hours, drain them, and see if they go back into the original container. This gives a rough *volume* check.

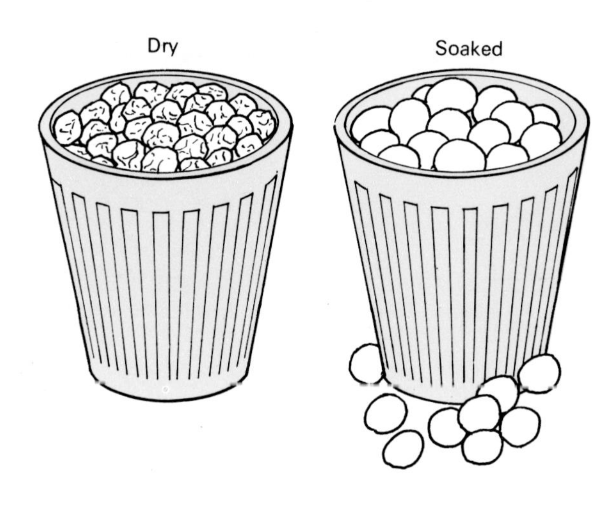

Displacement The exact volume of both dry and soaked peas can be found by displacement of water. One textbook method is shown here.

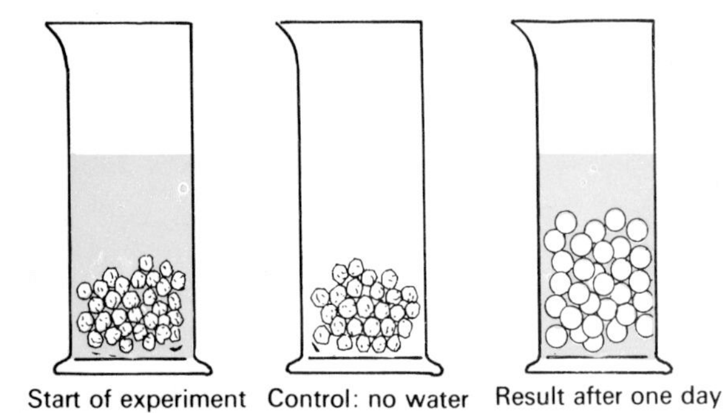

In practice, however, the peas often swell at the bottom of the jar until they are so tightly packed that not only is their full expansion impossible, but it is also extremely difficult to dig them out of the jar after the experiment is over. It is safer to proceed in the following way:

1 Measure the volume of some water, being sure to start with plenty.

2 Add the dry peas and measure the new total volume of peas and water together.

3 Soak the measured peas overnight.

4 Drain the soaked peas and add to the same volume of water as in the first stage.

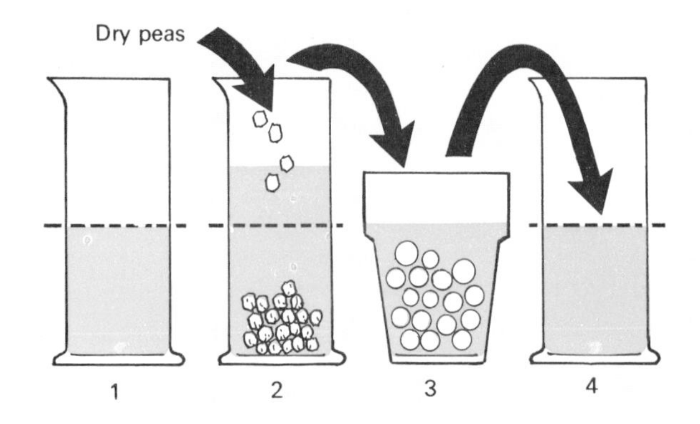

The volume of the dry peas is found accurately by noting how much the volume increases when the peas are added to the water in the measuring jar. The volume of the same peas after soaking is found in the same way.

This method of measuring volumes will be very useful later. The child who really understands this kind of technique has great advantages over the one who has to use such methods for the first time in the middle of an experiment dealing with some other concept.

Weight (or mass)

From the volume measurements of dry and soaked seeds, pupils will very probably guess or suggest their simple *weight* relationships, that is which are lighter and which are heavier.

If classroom apparatus is even only approximately accurate, test the simple hypothesis which pupils will be able to offer. Maybe some will go further.

A few practical details need to be considered, for example:

The soaked seeds should be drained and dabbed dry to avoid weighing drops of water.
Enough seeds need to be used to get reasonable results, say a hundred or more peas. (If several children count out twenty, this can be done very quickly.)

If the weighing can be carried out with standard weights, pupils can find out how much water has gone into the peas, and so on.

An interesting short project could begin with a 1-lb tin of processed peas.

Strain off the peas, count them, and make a rough estimate of the weight of dry peas which went into the 1 lb of the contents.

Are dry seeds or soaked seeds easier to study?

1 Take some dry peas, and some which have been soaked for not more than twenty-four hours and then drained (and dabbed dry if necessary).

Compare their appearance. Which shows more clearly such details as the oval white mark of the stalk, or the triangular root inside the skin?

2 On a piece of paper (a clean scrap will do) try carefully to take a dry pea and a soaked pea to pieces.

A cocktail stick, plastic or wooden, helps in the fine manipulation, and is far less of a problem in other ways than a pin or a compass point.

3 Try the same comparisons with maize. The pattern of the structures will be different, but the results of soaking will be similar.

4 A simple idea may be developing: 'Soaked seeds are easier to study than dry ones.'

If this idea is in the pupils' minds, test it together, using other kinds of seed—haricot, butter, red or blackeye beans, for example—sold in supermarkets for food.

5 Keeping records of growth and development

What is growth? Has the tall eight-year-old grown more than the fat eight-year-old (supposing they weigh the same)? What does 'grown-up' mean to a child, or to a grown-up?

Records of seedling height

Plant some seeds under favourable conditions, for instance in pots of well-dampened Vermiculite on a warm windowsill. It is interesting to have different sorts:

Peas, beans or sunflowers.
Maize, wheat or oats.

They pose different measurement problems, as well as illustrating different growth forms.

Begin recording the time (in days) immediately, even though the height measurement will be zero for several days. This shows an important point: the time-lag which children may not expect, but which every gardener recognizes.

What to measure

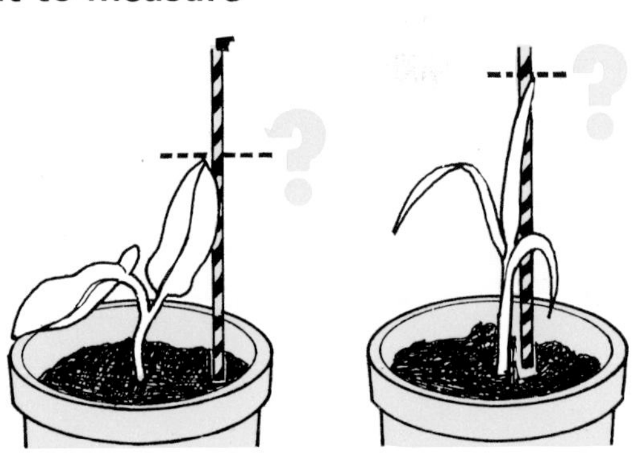

When the seedlings emerge, decide exactly what you are going to measure. For the first group of seedlings you could measure to the top of the stem from the soil level; and for the second group from soil level to the top of the leaf or to the top of the entire plant. It is probably best to measure to the top of the stem when there is one.

How to measure Will you:

Measure without disturbing?
Dig up a sample daily?
Sow daily so that you have a series always available?

Problems arise; you need a series of records, but each method has snags. With the first method, you may find it difficult to measure accurately because seedlings are often crowded together. Consider:

Putting your thumbnail as a marker on a vertical pencil and then measuring the distance with a ruler.
Using a marked straw, or a straw fitted with a sliding strip of card.

The special problem about digging up a sample every day is that it reduces your stock, and children are, and should be, unwilling to sacrifice their seedlings.

However, full observation of the growth of seedlings should naturally include the growth of roots. Some will grow against glass. This is convenient for observation, if not for setting up; but the box has to be made and in any case the method does not always work.

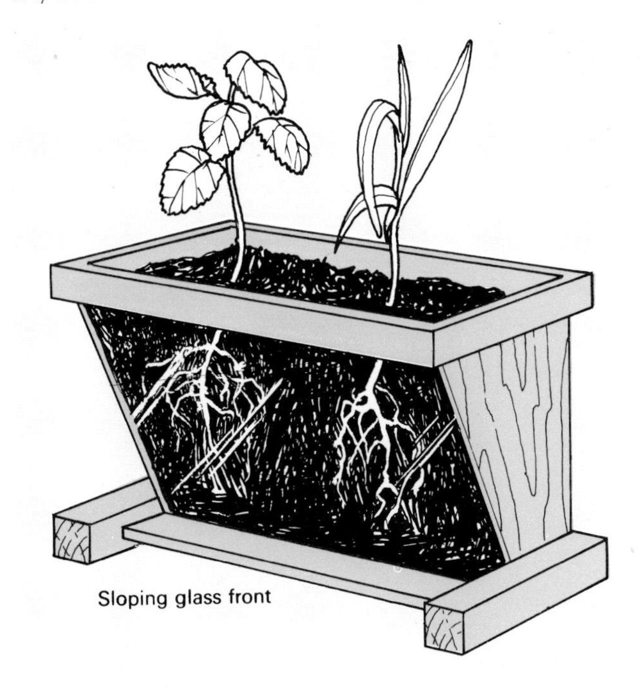

Sloping glass front

So you may have no option but to dig up seedlings. Get community spares planted in your own study group and by the pupils in the classroom. (This makes an excellent buffer activity for the quick pupils.) These spares may serve several purposes, for example as replacements, or as offerings to 'science'. Who will look after them?

Individuals or groups

How far is personal ownership an important factor with children in different age groups? Can one use class work to help children with different backgrounds to develop a community spirit?

Three hands are often needed for activities such as measuring seedling heights and organizing supports for taller plants. Does it work better to have:

Permanent pairs or casual assistance?
Friendship pairing or organized grouping—boy and girl, quick and slow, etc?

How far can the organization of children into groups for activities be in its own right a scientific experiment on the part of the teacher or student?

Measuring and recording how far seedlings have grown and developed need to be done individually, as well as combined into a form of group record, in order to be valuable scientifically. Why? What problems can group records help to solve? How can children be helped to see their value? (See bibliography: 15.)

Cooperative work by pupils makes it essential for the teacher to think hard about the progress of the individual pupils. What work should you see from each child? And what should you record in the way of special interests, difficulties, home help, and so on?

Making the record How can you transfer the measured height to some form of record?

How do you rate the usefulness of block diagrams as compared with columns of figures?

Some children may wish to use a representational method, by doing a drawing that represents a seedling, life-size, at first; they will probably change their minds later.

Other suggestions, which involve non-representational methods of recording, are:

One sheet of paper for each kind of seedling.
Alternate strips of paper on a block diagram (for comparison), with two kinds of seedling.
Paint, sticky paper, sticky labels, crayons, etc.

What scale do you find appropriate? One idea is a scale in days, along the bottom of a graph.

How will you organize the record to allow for irregularities: weekends, forgetfulness, the deaths of seedlings, etc? You could leave gaps for days when no measurements are made.

Arrange for an accurate record of height against days, even if there are no values for some of the days. These can be estimated once the measured values are recorded, and this is valuable as a method (interpolation).

Children measuring seedlings stuck with Sellotape on the record

A representation of the record (gaps are weekends)

Length of record The measuring activity needs to go on for at least a week, and preferably for two or three weeks, to get good records; the longer the better, while the plants are well cared for, and the children are not bored.

Keep your records of height, either for one plant or for the average height of one set of seedlings.

Unexpected results How can you avoid unintended differences in conditions, such as a cold or a hot spell? Perhaps it doesn't matter so long as the special changes are recorded; they may well explain special results.

Darkness Try putting some of the same sorts of seeds in the dark, to compare their growth in height with those grown in the light. Devise conditions that are as far as possible the same. Children appreciate fairness in experiments. How will you organize darkness? Could you use black paper cones or a cupboard? What other conditions, besides the amount of light, will be changed? Is temperature, for example, affected?

Predict, and let your pupils predict also, what the effect of darkness might be, and then test the predictions. If several different predictions are forthcoming, this is good, since there will then be no sharp division between those children who are 'right' and those who are 'wrong'.

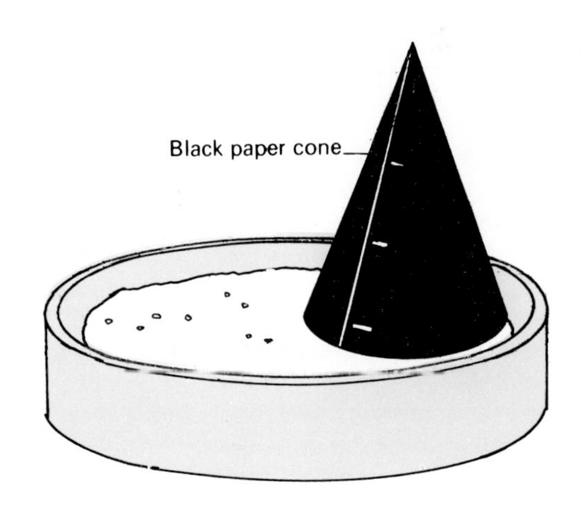

Maintaining interest The most important thing is not to let measuring become mechanical. Compare what the children's seeds have done with what the seed packets say, or with what their garden experience tells them. Note: the seed of the tallest tree in the world (*Sequoia gigantea*) measures 2 × 8 *millimetres*. Use this fact! You might also consult the *Guinness Book of Records*, which gives the heights of these trees.

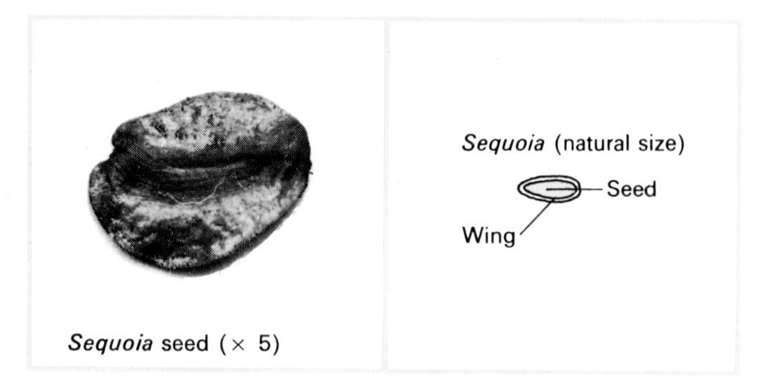

Sequoia seed (× 5)

For further adult-level investigation get hold of M.K. Sands' excellent little book *Problems in Plant Physiology* Chapter 2 deals shortly but intelligently with dormancy, germination and growth curves, measurement criteria and environmental factors in plant growth.

See bibliography : 27.

Objectives

Consider the following Science 5/13 Objectives for children learning science. To what extent do you find your pupils' abilities fit into this framework?

Ability to use representational symbols for recording information on charts or block graphs.
Ability to tabulate information and use tables.
Ability to use non-representational symbols in plans, charts, etc.
Ability to interpret observations in terms of trends and rates of change.
Ability to use histograms and other simple graphical forms for communicating data.
Ability to select the graphical form most appropriate to the information being recorded.

Measuring the growth of lawn seedlings

Now test a householder's problem: the lawn.

Grow grass seedlings from new grass seed in a tray (or similar container), in good light. Old grass seed is very disappointing.

Method When the grass has grown a bit, measure (approximately) the height of the crop, and then with scissors cut half to the level of the top edge of the tray. Note the approximate length of the cut grass.

Keep this up, 'mowing' at specified intervals and measuring the grass clippings to get a rough average. Keep a record and a running total. If measuring length is too difficult, try filling a small standard measure (eg a marked egg-cup) with the clippings to see how much grass actually grows.

Would weighing the total clippings be possible with the balances available in the classroom? Would weight (mass) be more, or less, useful than length as a measurement?

When you have measured the lengths, compare the running total with the height (above tray level) of the uncut grass before it begins to fall over. This could show whether mown grass grows more than uncut grass.

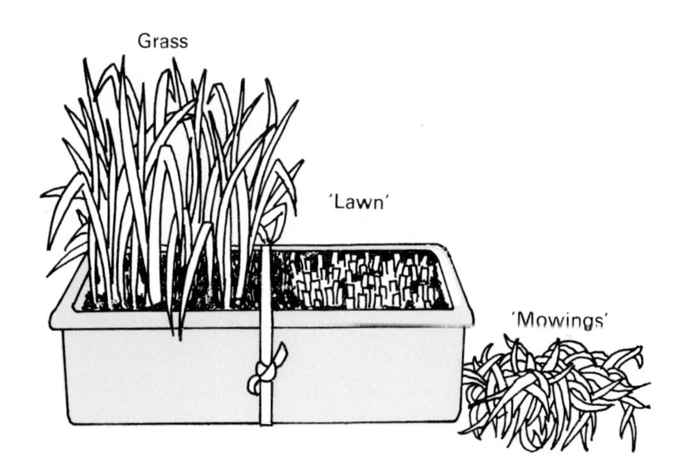

Wider considerations Try the treatment on mustard or cress. What happens?

Consider grass as a crop and as animal food. What other plants would put up with mowing or grazing treatment?

This experiment has wide social and economic significance. What would happen if grass ceased to grow as it does?

There are many points of contact with other subject areas here, for example:

The local fields (if any).
Hay and haymaking.
Food for different kinds of animals.
Grasslands of the world.

Growth, change and development

Seedlings may grow. A few seeds may change without growing: for example, they may go mouldy. Seedlings which grow will also develop, which is a different phenomenon.

Seeds change into *seedlings* which change into *plants.*
What is there to record?
How is the best way to do it so that children can identify the processes?

1 Closely observe some fast-developing seeds, for example mustard, in a covered dish on a damp surface. Look for cracked skin, young root, first leaves, etc.

When will you begin dated records? How do you define (recognize) germination day? How will you organize a seed-record diary?

This close observation is a truly scientific activity, and adults as well as children learn to do it more thoroughly and more accurately by conscious practice. Noticing changes can become a kind of competition.

2 Watch the growth and development stages of your chosen type of plant. Why should you use only one type of plant for one piece of work? In the figure these two seedlings from the same kind of seed are not identical; how would you characterize the differences here? Which has grown more? Which shows more advanced development?

3 When measurement of the height of seedlings is under way, more attention can be given to development, such as the number of leaves per plant. This works well with fast-growing weeds observed outside the school building, as well as with classroom specimens.

4 Choose some way of recording the development of a seedling: perhaps a label on the graphic height record, giving the number of leaves.

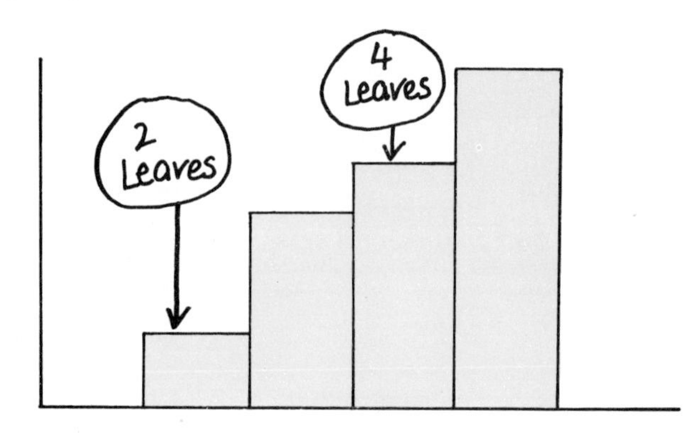

How else could this record be shown satisfactorily? What sort of progression does it, or might it, show? How could the arrival of flower buds and open flowers (eg on pea plants) be recorded? Will the development, say of new leaves or of flowers, make any difference to the rate of growth?

Hollyhocks in the school garden provide excellent material for summer-term research here into the growth in height, the number and size of leaves, and the production of flowers.

5 Differences between growth and development can be clearly demonstrated by simple classroom experiments, for instance, by sowing a few scattered mustard seeds in a tray of damp sand, sawdust or Vermiculite, and covering some of the seeds completely with a small black paper cone. This is not airtight (as a pot might be) but simply keeps the seeds or seedlings in the dark (see page 19). Simple sketches probably give the best records of the results.

How could, should, or do you help pupils to see the difference between the two concepts of *growth* (in stem height) and *development* (in, say, the number of leaves)? Do any of them suggest the idea spontaneously?

Any insects available (eg caterpillars) or other metamorphosing creatures (eg tadpoles) would make a valuable, though not too easy, comparison. Can you think of other examples?

6 Children's interest: starting points

Looking at the internal structure of peanuts

Children are almost always interested in something which can be *eaten* in class, with or without teacher approval.

They are almost always interested, too, in things which will *belong to them personally* (the 'Can I take it home?' pattern).

They usually enjoy the *unusual* or unexpected, as long as it poses no threat.

Given reasonable weather, work which takes pupils *out of the classroom* usually appeals. With seeds and seedlings we can have all of these starting points.

Seeds for all Choose seeds whose internal structure can easily be discovered. A good choice would be peanuts, in their shells for at least part of the exercise.

Get your own peanuts, and a magnifier; they are really worth careful study, outside and inside, detail by detail.

Some children will be very ready to cooperate over looking at the shell carefully, splitting it into halves, seeing the silver-white 'satin' lining, observing the two seeds 'like twins in a cradle', etc. Many have immediate thoughts of cracking and eating, but can usually wait to the end of the lesson.

Here is a temptation being put in front of pupils. How far can, and should, you be rigid about not eating the nuts until permission is given, and how many spares should you provide?

Seedlings for all If each child is to have a seedling, you must choose materials which can really be free for all. Mustard fulfills several requirements, maybe even the making of tiny, sample sandwiches with minute pieces of bread and butter on a Friday afternoon.

What will children need besides cheap or free pots, a growing medium and cheap, easily obtained seeds?

Perhaps one crop for continued 'science' (observation, measurement, etc) would be useful, and another in self-contained units for tasting or taking home.

Using the unusual A cress seed has a special unusual characteristic: the outside layer becomes gelatinous and sticky when soaked in water. Try:

Soaking the seeds to see this layer.
Planting some cress seeds in odd (damp) places, such as on a plastic sponge or porous clay standing up out of water.

Planting some cress seeds on a rough damp surface, like half a brick, which can be inverted after germination to 'tease' the seedlings. (Notice the root-hairs.)

Invent your own planting surface.

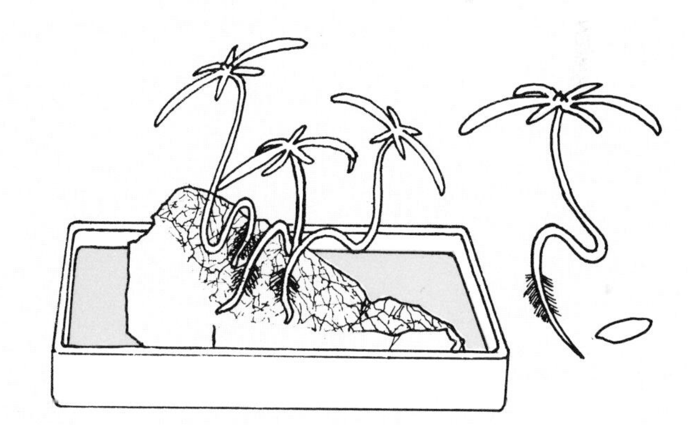

Going outside the classroom How do seeds travel? How have seedlings come to the places where you find them?

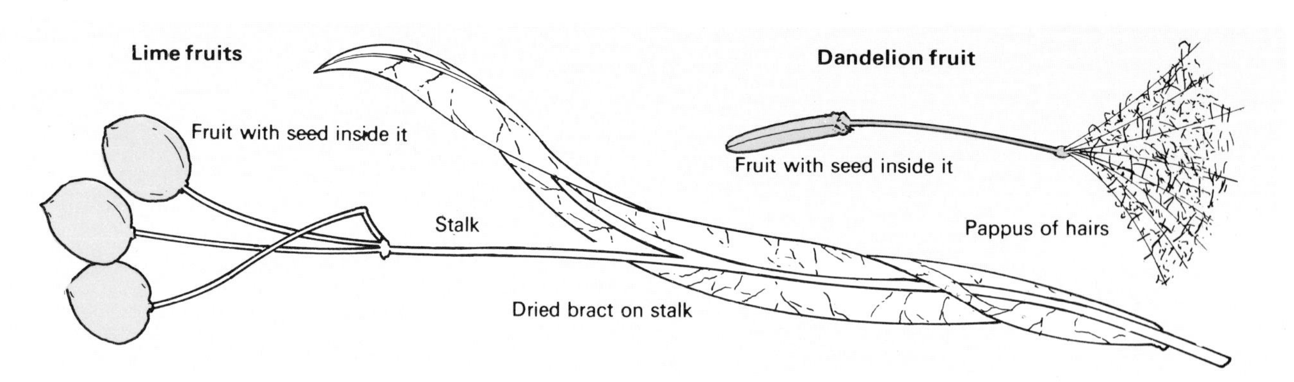

The cracks in the pavement against garden walls or houses often provide just enough space, soil and water for seedlings to grow. A search around the most arid school playground will almost certainly produce some examples, such as willowherb, dandelion, groundsel, and even small trees such as sycamore or birch. Crazy paving may have hawthorn or willow seedlings coming up 'unplanted'. (See bibliography: 6, 7, 19.)

The distribution methods of all the common wind-scattered seeds and fruits, eg sycamore 'propellers' ash 'keys', etc, can be tested by the pupils themselves.

How far can, and should, children's spontaneous interests be used to help them towards social behaviour and self-discipline, or scientific discovery?

7 The value of collections

Seeds, pips or stones?

Seeds are among the most collectable objects in primary school science; collecting can easily, and usefully, be extended to include pictures from seed catalogues and seed packets, frozen food packets and can labels. The more examples one has of a specific kind of material, the better one is able to form a general idea.

1 Look at all the illustrations of peas you can find, and at real peas as they come from grocers, supermarkets or greengrocers.

Some are in pods. (Some young children will certainly not know that peas all started that way.) What other seeds come in pods? Is this a pod?

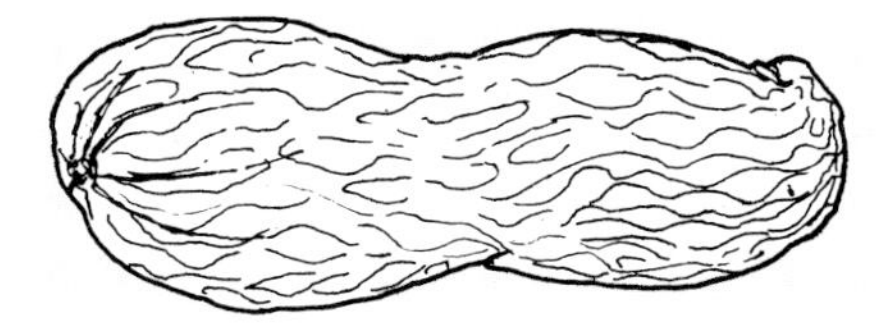

Compare pea-pods with the cases of peanuts. Compare a pea and a peanut. How do the seeds compare? Should they be in the same group?

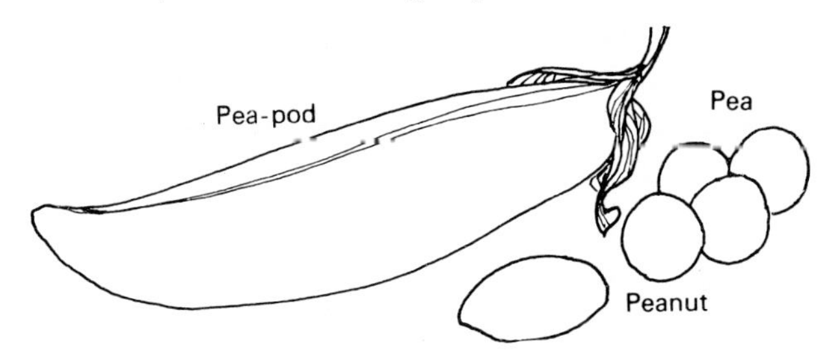

Group (classify) runner beans, broad beans, etc, adding other labels.

2
a. Collect and look at all the pictures, can labels, etc, of things with pips in them such as apples, tomatoes, raspberries and grapefruit. Some, but not too many, of the real things will help.

b. Add fruits with stones, such as plums, cherries or prunes, and crack the stones (with nutcrackers rather than hammers, if these are available).

c. Compare apple, orange or grapefruit pips with various fruit stones, especially by taking them to pieces.

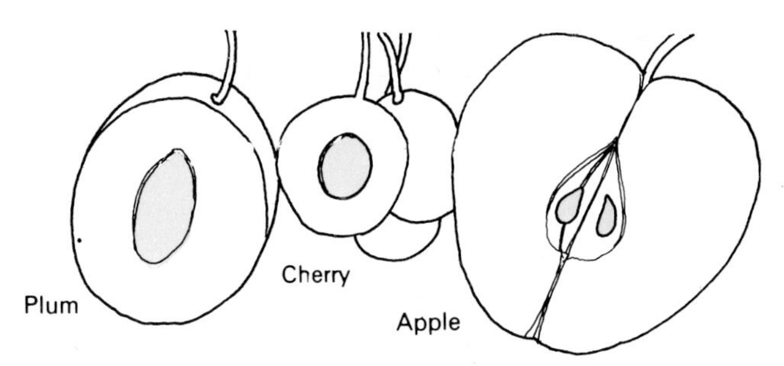

What factors are common to all the fruits in your collection? What differences of structure do you find? Consider:

One seed/many seeds.
Stone/no stone round the seed.
Hard pips/soft (unripe) pips.

Group them.

How do the examples in (*b*) and (*c*) extend the idea of fruits having seeds inside them?

3 Collect and look at as many fruit-tin labels as you can find. Add fruit-juice labels, and packet-pictures of sultanas, grapes, dates, etc. Add (real, or in pictures) melons, tomatoes, cucumbers and marrows.

What are pips? 'Will they grow into new plants?' is the basic question. Pips are all *inside* something else, so this can be taken a step further. Is the content of the stone a pip? Can one make a class of juicy fruits with pips in them? What does this comparison say about pips, stones and seeds? Can one say 'A fruit is something with one or more seeds (pips) inside it'?

How far can looking at everyday objects (eg packets and labels) lead to greater knowledge and understanding of scientific facts?

Start with nos 1, 2 or 3, and see how the other activities link on. An excellent collage could result.

Seeds or grains?

1 Collect a large and varied selection of seed-pods, pictures of pods, fruits with pips inside, etc. Alternatively, review what has already been collected. Peanuts in shells, tomatoes, apples and poppy-heads make clear what one expects of seeds: that they will be produced inside fruits.

2 Next collect together acorns, hazelnuts, ash 'keys', dandelion 'parachutes', sunflower 'seeds', etc. Peel, crack or skin one example of each (if possible) and investigate the contents.

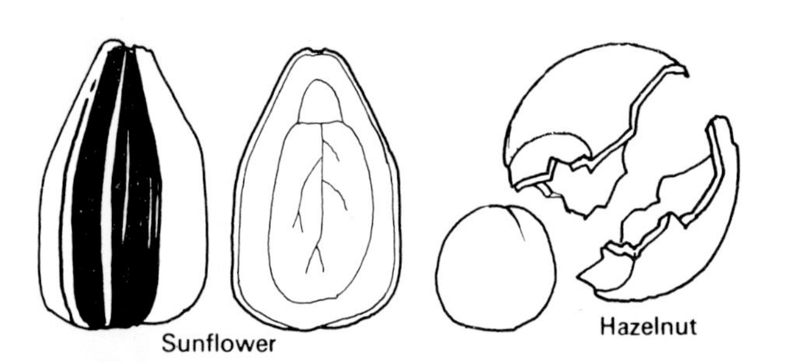

Each of these contains a single *seed* but the outer skin (hazelnut shell, black or white sunflower skin, etc) makes it into a *fruit*. Can you find the essentials (embryo and food stores) in each?

Using soaked seeds (preferably soaked for not more than twenty-four hours), investigate internal structures, perhaps with a lens and a large pin, and note your observations. This activity, done thoughtfully, should produce valuable classification data. Peanuts, apple pips, beans and peas are very good.

3 Now tackle some grains—oats, wheat, barley and maize—and check with textbook illustrations (eg Mackean's *Introduction to Biology*, for wheat). Soak, peel, carefully dissect (with magnifier) and identify the food store and the embryo which would eventually have used it.

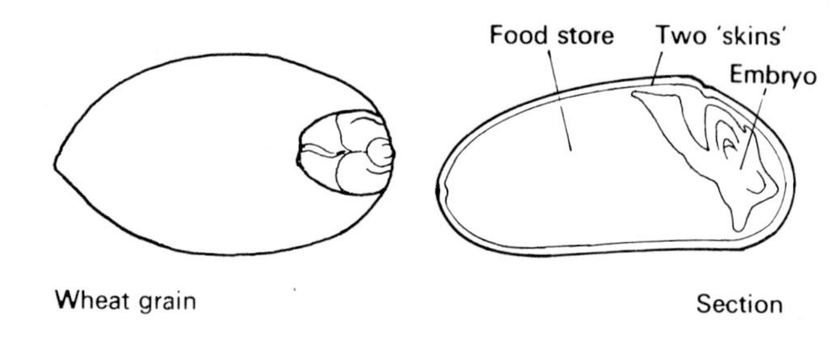

Are there any seed-pods? No. But the grains grow into plants, so they must have a seed in each. However, they seem to be fruits too. Consider no.1: an apple comes from an apple flower, a poppy-head from a poppy flower, etc; and nos 2 and 3: each hazelnut or maize grain comes from a single hazel or maize flower.

See bibliography: 21, 22.

4 Growing the seeds and fruits from nos 1 and 2 alongside the grains from no. 3 makes clear the big difference between grains and the rest: they produce quite different kinds of seedling.

Consider all the grain plants; what are their wild relations? Wild oats are a kind of grass and are a problem for farmers.

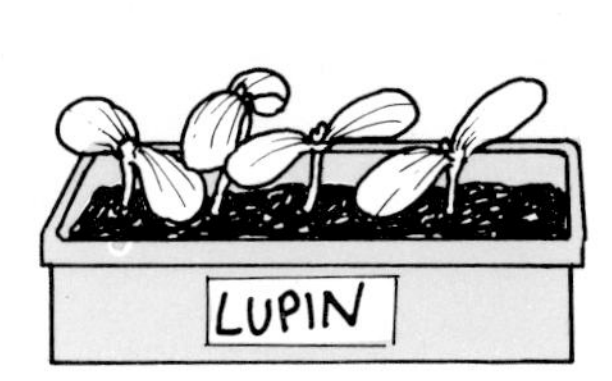

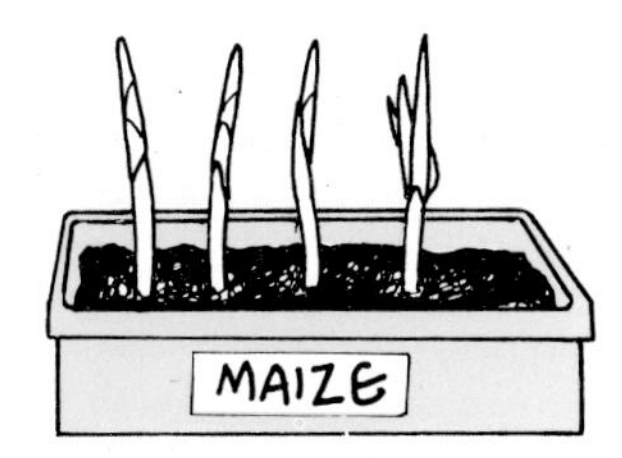

Grow two little 'fields' in similar trays of soil, such as compost or Vermiculite: one of lupins and the other of maize. Let the children notice all the differences they can.

The lupin and maize seedlings could well be planted out into gardens or pots after two or three weeks; they are worth growing on.

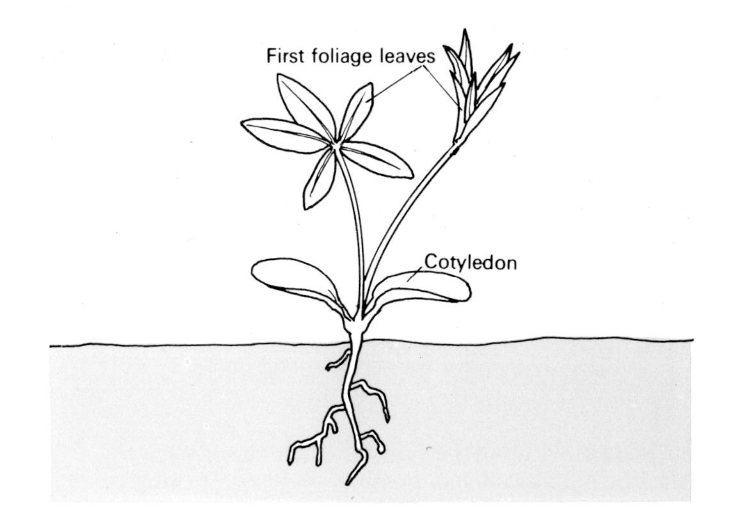

8 Children and vocabulary

Do we need words to be able to understand things, or are words only needed for communication?

1 Inspect an unopened peanut shell closely. Try to describe it as exactly as possible. Are any of these words useful or necessary here: shell, case or pod; ridges or veins; 'beak' end or stalk end? Rattle the shell, predict how many nuts are inside. Open it carefully.

2 Compare it with an ordinary pea-pod, or with the picture from a can or a seed catalogue showing pea-pods. A peanut shell, containing nuts, is technically a *fruit*; is this (in this context) a useful word? How does the idea of peanuts in a shell link up with peas in a pod?

3 Look for a pea-pod, real or in a picture, with the remains of the flower attached.

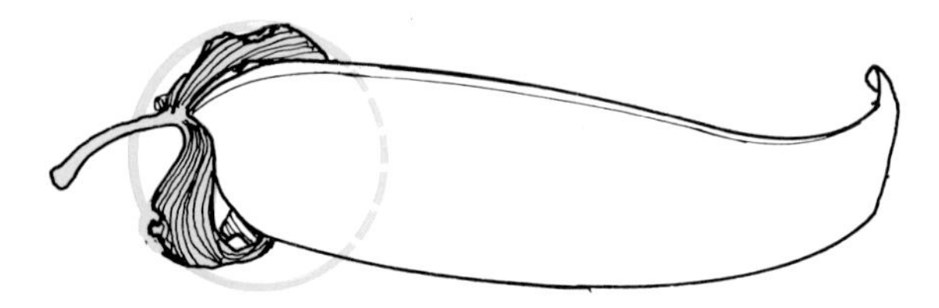

If pea-pods have come from flowers, maybe pods come from flowers, horse-chestnuts come from flowers, and apples come from flowers. This might lead to the idea that fruits come from flowers.

Find as many examples as possible; the plant which shows both flowers and fruits at the same time is most convincing. What words are needed for the description of, and discussion about, fruits? Can one manage without the botany textbook terminology?

4 Skin a peanut seed. Peel a soaked pea, bean, an apple pip, etc. The seed-skin round each is technically the *testa*; is this name helpful?

5 Carefully separate the parts of a peanut, a pea, a bean and an apple pip. Between the two 'halves' find the small root and leaves of the future plant, the embryo. Separate it from its food stores and look with a magnifier.

The two halves containing food stores in each seed are technically *cotyledons*; at what stage in science (and literacy) would you use this term?

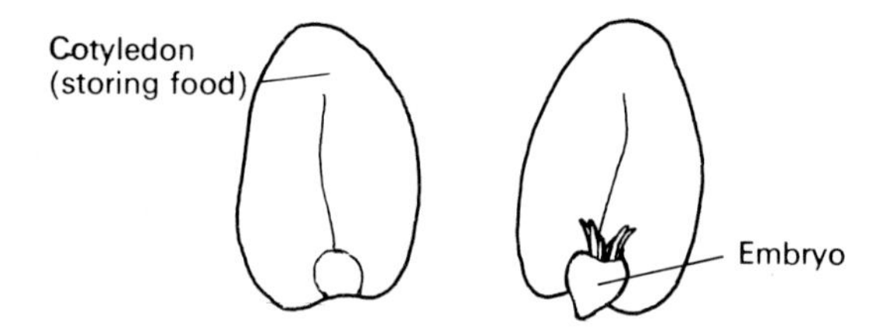

The seeds listed above (peanuts, peas, etc) are technically *dicotyledons*; when would you consider this term useful?

Is the word *embryo* perhaps important, even with young children? In what other contexts is it important?

6 Look for embryos in seeds.

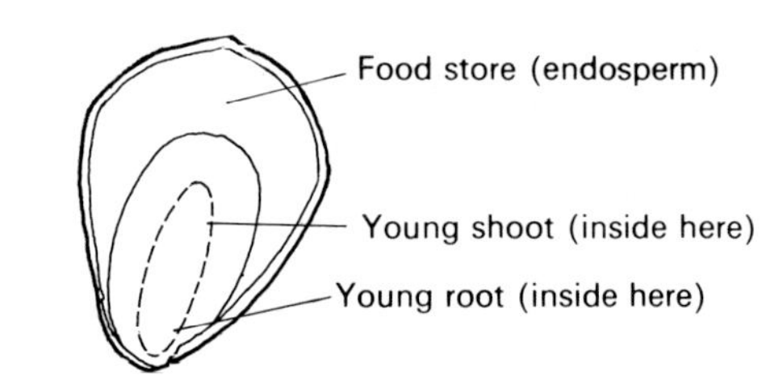

This can be extended very well to sycamore and sunflower fruits, acorns and horse-chestnuts. Dissecting grains, such as maize or wheat, to identify their structure, is more difficult. While you do it, test different methods.

At what stage would you expect to teach that grain plants are technically *monocotyledons*, and that the food store in the grain is called the *endosperm*?

How far do you find that children are helped by simple descriptive words, and how far by less common technical ones?

Consider the following Objectives from Science 5/13. How far do your pupils' abilities fit this framework?

Ability to use new words appropriately.
Ability to discuss and record impressions of living and non-living things in the environment.
Appreciation of the need to learn the meaning of new words and to use them correctly.
Familiarity with names of living things and non-living materials.
Enjoyment in examining ambiguity in the use of words.
Preference for using words correctly.

9 Explaining, predicting and testing

What do seeds need?

Water and air Here is a transcript of a tape-recorded conversation between a teacher and some children aged eight:

Teacher: 'Why do you think the seeds in the soil didn't come up?'
Child: 'Some weren't watered and some were. There was four in a group and three came up and one of them disappeared.'
Teacher: 'Did you grow any seeds?'
Child: 'Yes.'
Teacher: 'What happened to yours?'
Child: 'Nothing.'
Teacher: 'Didn't they come up?'
Child: 'No.'
Teacher: 'Why do you think that was?'
Child: 'They probably didn't have any water as well.'
Teacher: 'You think you didn't water them enough?'
Child: 'Yes.'
Teacher: 'Do you think water is the most important thing then?'
Child: 'Yes . . . . No.'
Teacher: 'What do you think is the most important?'
Child: 'Air.'
Teacher: 'How could you find out if plants grow if they don't have air?'
Child: 'Bury them; Miss — soaked peas in water overnight and then she brought them to the class and she put some in a jar without a lid on, and some in a jar with a lid on, and then we waited a while—about a week—and most of them in the jar without a lid started to grow but some had tried to grow in the jar with the lid on, but they just died away.'
Teacher: 'Well, didn't you have any air in the jar with the lid on?'
Child: 'No, because we closed it tight.'
Teacher: 'If you had this jar in the room it would be full of air, wouldn't it?'
Child: 'Yes.'
Teacher: 'Then you put the lid on. It was still full of air, wasn't it?'
Child: 'Yes.'
Teacher: 'So, why didn't they grow?'
Child: 'Because the peas had already used the air up.'
Teacher: 'They used the air up? How did they use the air up?'
Child: 'Well, they could suck it up . . . into them.'
Teacher: 'How do they do this?'
Child: 'Well, like they suck up water. They drink water, they must use air like we use air. If we went in a room and it had been full of air, we would use it all up.'
Teacher: 'You think that they use up the air the same way as we use up the air?'
Child: 'Yes.'

Sort out all the children's ideas of plant needs, and set up simple experiments to test their suggestions as rigorously as you can. Children can be helped to do just this kind of thinking and testing, especially if they find adults taking the exercise (and the children themselves) seriously.

A favourable environment Here is a transcript of another conversation with a different group of children:

Lecturer: 'What do we need to make a seed grow?'
Julian: 'Some water and earth.'
Lecturer: 'What do you think? Do you agree?'
Sarah: 'No, I don't agree. You have water, light . . .'
Lecturer: 'Julian said earth. Do you agree with that?'
Sarah: 'No, I don't. We grew them in jars with blotting

paper and no earth, and they grew.'
Colin: 'You can have water, light and heat, and sometimes you can have blotting paper. You can have it on its own without earth.'
Lecturer: 'You both said you need light. Do you think you need light to make it grow?'
Sarah: 'Well, some plants—you can put them in a cupboard and they will grow.'
Lecturer: 'What about the seeds? Do the seeds really need light at all?'
Colin: 'No. Most seeds are usually under soil—they don't really have light.'

Study exactly what the children said first, and how the lecturer's questions gave them stimulus and time to think further and improve their answers.

Which of these children's answers are certainly based on classroom experience, and which on general knowledge? The children were beginning to sort out their ideas gained from experimental evidence but not previously used in a conscious way. How could they now be helped to *test* that early idea that light is necessary for seeds to grow?

In some cases it is true that light is necessary, for instance for some varieties of lettuce. What were the children really thinking about when they said that light was needed?

In the second transcript Julian and Colin state their ideas of a *favourable environment* for germination. Is it feasible to test all the conditions which might be involved? A further discussion with pupils would help them to imagine the conditions in which different seeds and crops do actually grow. This could stimulate research projects of three kinds:

Experiments.
Using books
Interviewing farmers, gardeners, etc.

How can you enlarge the idea of the *favourable and unfavourable environment* for plant life, and for animal and human life? Perhaps you could use pairs of pictures: for example, of deserts and tropical forests, and of the Arctic and fields. Children are not always ready to consider plants, particularly seeds, as living things. When they have had a little experience of owning and caring for seedlings, they may become so enthusiastic that they start to think of seedlings in the same way as pets, needing warmth, and so on, and they may overdo it.

What questions and what materials (eg pictures of alpine plants in snow, or cacti in a desert), can you use to help them? How far can you combine such second-hand evidence with tests that use real seeds and seedlings?

Consider the suggestion that 'The best questions are those which test ideas against real materials; the worst are those which demand a "learnt" right or wrong answer.'

With pupils' own experiments and experiences in mind, look very critically at summaries with all the stock answers, like inside the covers of the Ladybird book *Plants and How They Grow*. At what stage, if at all, should this method of instruction be used?

See bibliography: 4.

Soil, sun and water Here is a transcript of a conversation with children aged between eight and ten:

Teacher: 'Here is this great big plant. Where does all the stuff—or the food—come from which has come to make this?
Children: 'The water and the soil.'
Melanie (aged ten): 'Well, it's hard to know where it could come from because there is no proof that it has—wherever you say it has come from. Because somebody could say it comes from the soil, another could say it's from the sun, another that it comes from the water, but nobody really knows, do they?'

Test Melanie's ideas as far as possible, using:

Seedlings with and without soil.
Seedlings with and without sun.

One of Melanie's ideas is virtually impossible to test fairly in classroom conditions. Exactly why is this?

Tests Are you testing only one kind of seedling? Or will you try, say, beans, cress, maize, grass and others (that is, large and small seeds, and large and small grains)? Melanie's was a bean plant. Is it more important to cut down the total number of variables (and therefore choices), or to test several kinds of seed under controlled conditions? What other conditions could be changed in such tests?

In a laboratory, you can take the question further than would be possible (or desirable) with junior children. For example, you can chop up some young plants, weigh them, dry them over boiling water, and weigh them again. (Subtracting the second weight from the first gives the weight of *water* in the seedlings.)

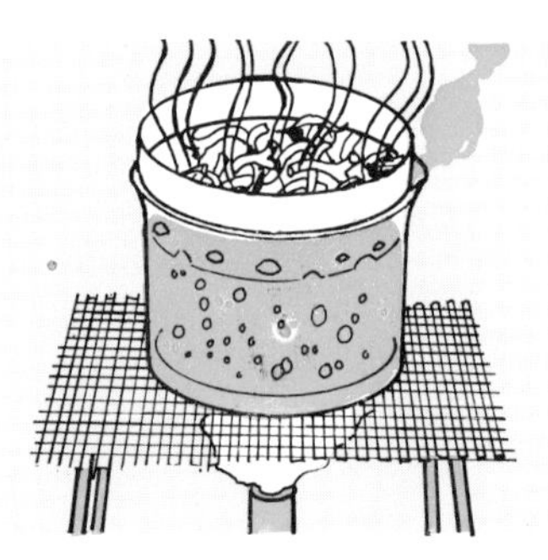

The second weighing gives the weight of *dry* material; if this weight is compared with the weight of an equal number of seeds (dry) one can test Melanie's third suggestion.

How can, and do, you help children with the following?

Thinking out their own explanations about where plant material comes from.
Working out ways in which they could test them practically.

What will seeds become?

Recognition Look at seed packets with pictures of plants, eg mustard, cress and beans. How do you *know* that the kind of plant from these seeds will be predictable? How does a child get to know?

Try some prepared recognition problems. Offer an adult trays of seedlings of cress and wheat mixed, cress and mustard mixed, and a third containing wheat, oats and maize. (This last one can be difficult.)

Children will like to sow their first-name initials with one kind of seed in a dish of seeds of another kind, using a sandwich box or soup plate of damp Vermiculite. Can they see their initials among the seedlings?

Looking at cress seeds through a magnifier; mustard seedlings are seen on the left, cress seedlings on the right

Comparison Compare similar looking seeds, eg melon and marrow seeds, sunflower fruits, apple pips. Then as far as possible collect the fruits and pictures of these, and also of the plants and trees. (Seed packets help.)

How could you, and how could children, best exhibit the apparent similarity of the seed starting points, and the differences in the products? (The seeds *are* distinguishable, and once you know, you know.)

Behaviour Seed and seedling behaviour may also be predictable: try loosely rolling five maize grains, all the same way up, in a folded, dampened paper handkerchief; repeat with wheat, oats, sunflowers, etc. Stand the rolls carefully in a coffee beaker, with a *little* water at the bottom, and enclose in a small plastic bag with a tie.

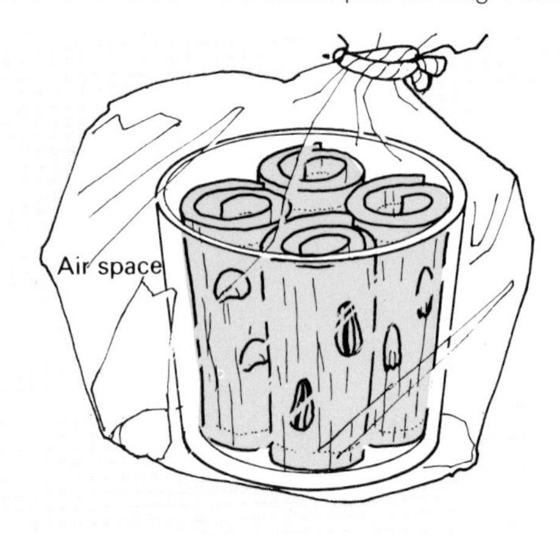

Inspect 3-7 days later and compare sets.

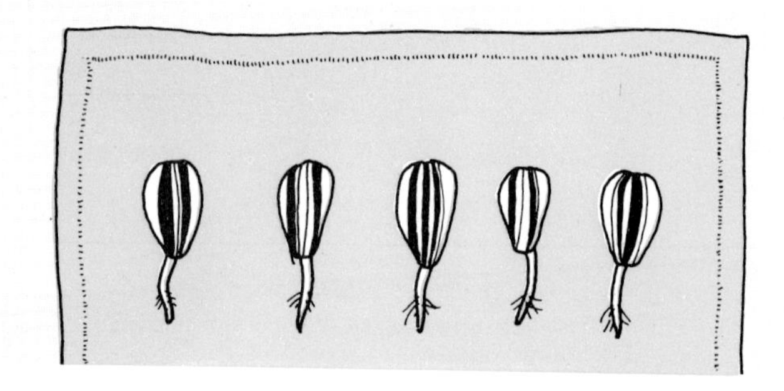

What about the behaviour of seeds which fall or are planted upside down? Set up another experiment with more than one kind of seed or grain, and place some or all of them upside down. Test every prediction made.

Predict (and later get children to predict) what will happen. Perhaps they won't grow at all, or perhaps they will grow the wrong way, or . . . ?

What is the general result?

What would happen to the seedling (if there were one) whose root went on growing upwards?

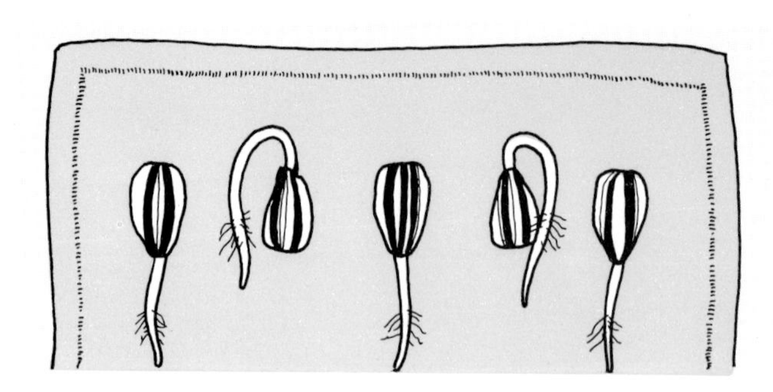

What about the seedling which gets turned upside down after it has started growing? Predict and test with cress. The seeds stick conveniently.

The inheritance of similar structures and similar behaviour has been fundamental throughout the history of life on earth, but it is also vital that offspring are not identical with their parents. Do you agree? If so, why? If not, why not?

Seedlings into plants: life cycles

Much of the material, such as seedlings, on which children work in school is soon thrown away. Is this educationally sound? How far can ideals and pressures be satisfied? How can long-term results, and therefore concepts, be achieved?

Growing in pots With the life cycle in mind, grow some chosen kinds of seed, eg French beans, dwarf peas and mustard, and some flower seeds such as dwarf nasturtiums, all of which are small enough to spend their entire life in a pot. Think about the following:

What size should the pots be? Should they be plastic? Should you use saucers?
What about space? A flat roof? The corridor windowsill? A greenhouse?
Do the seeds need nutrients such as Baby Bio? (Only a few drops are needed.)

Growing in the garden If at all possible use or establish a patch of school garden; the chess board pattern, described on page 50 of Science 5/13 *Early experiences*, is excellent if there is enough space for concrete between beds. What advantages and disadvantages does a real garden have? Are there any opportunities here for environmental study? What mathematical and social education may children develop from using such a garden?

See bibliography: 10, 16, 17.

Choose 'good' seeds, dip in dilute bleach to discourage moulds, germinate under optimum conditions, and plant out. Sow similar seeds direct in the garden (or pots) for comparing rates of growth, of leaf development and so on.

Where will you plant the runner beans? How will you organize holiday care? What can be gained from this work which is hardly possible in a classroom or laboratory?

Make a collage of real objects and pictures to illustrate this very important concept of the *life cycle* for one species.

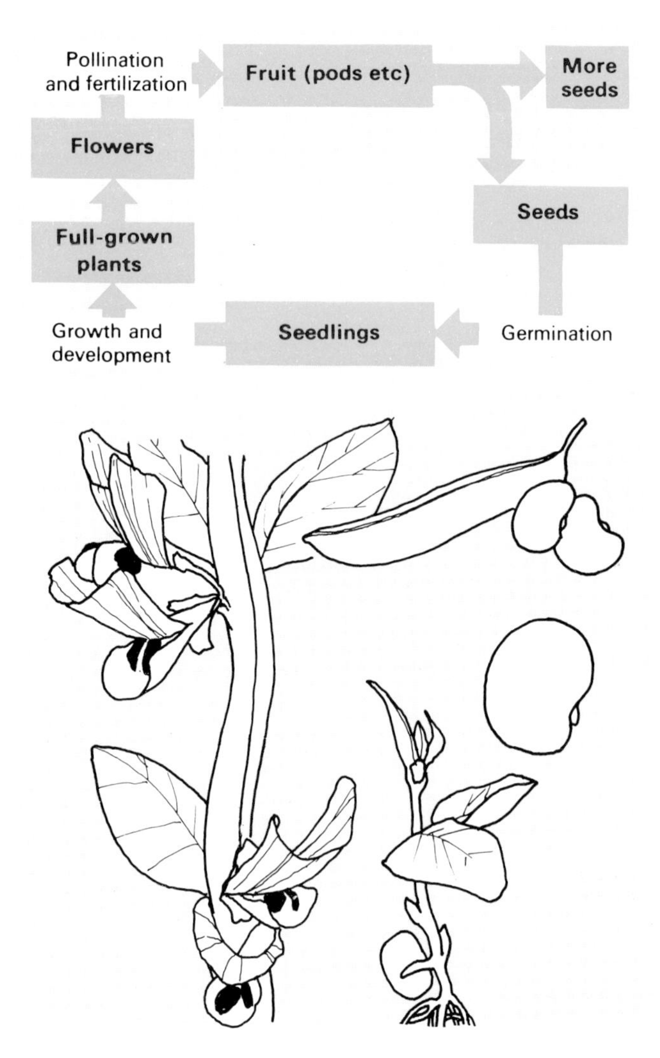

Other activities Children are more likely to be interested in our uses of plants at different stages than in the 'pure' life cycle.

They will be able to suggest and illustrate extensions, such as the use of plants for wine, flour, hay, furniture, wreaths, etc, and will enjoy being inventive. The life cycle will bring them back to the importance of plant life at every stage. (See bibliography: 20.)

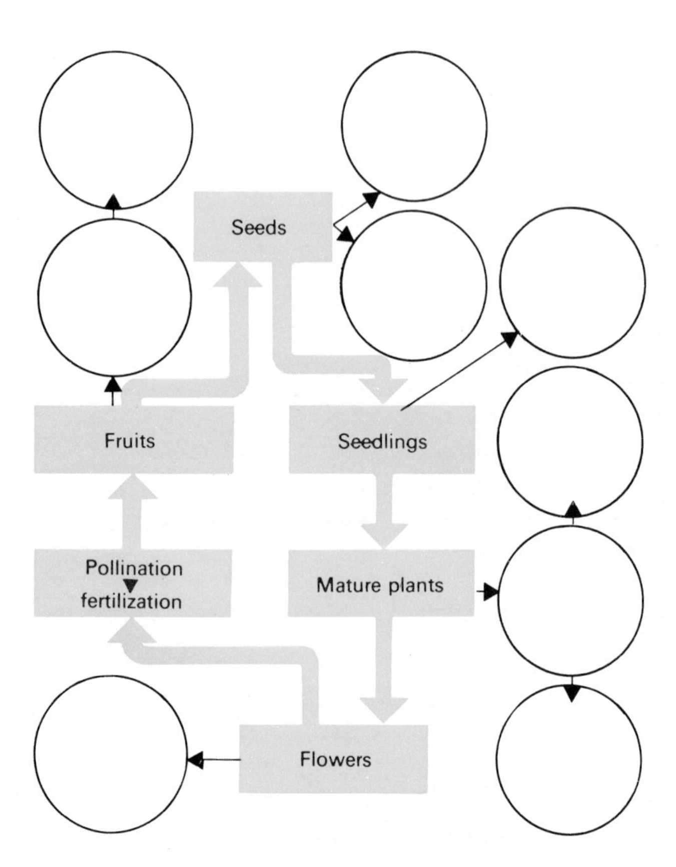

10 Science and everyday life: seeds and grains as food

Collect a display of seeds and grains used for food, and also pictures and labels.

Add materials and illustrations of food products (such as rye bread and popcorn) made from seeds and grains. What can be learnt from supermarkets and seed catalogues? Colleagues and children from abroad may have many other suggestions.

Some names need sorting out, for instance, the American 'corn' is the English 'maize'. Children may need help to recognize names.

How important are seeds and grains to the world? A good way to show food grains and their relevance is to organize visual material using production figures from the United Nations' Food and Agriculture Organization. Here are some ideas.

Draw a block diagram showing world production of food grains, with samples so that children know what the words mean and what other children in the world actually eat.

Make a collage on a world map to show production of the main crops. Even on an A4 map one grain could be stuck in the appropriate area for each 10 million tons. The really big producers can be seen in the table below.

World production in 1971 (10 million tons)	
Wheat	34
Maize	30
Rice	30
Barley	15
Oil 'seeds' (linseeds, sunflower, etc)	11
Millet (and sorghum)	10
Oats	6
Peas, beans, etc	4
Rye	3

World production in 1971 (10 million tons)	
Wheat	
USSR	9
USA	4
China	3
India	2
France	
Canada	
Turkey	
Italy	1 each
Australia	
W. Germany	
Pakistan	
Rice	
China	10
India	6
Indonesia	2
Pakistan	2
Japan	
Thailand	
Vietnam	1 each
Burma	
Brazil	

World production in 1971 (10 million tons)	
Maize	
USA	14
Brazil	
USSR	
Argentina	
Mexico	
France	1 each
South Africa	
Romania	
Yugoslavia	
India	
Barley	
USSR	4
Canada	
USA	1 each
France	
UK	
Millet	
USA	2
India	2
Nigeria	1

World production in 1971 (10 million tons)	
Oats	
USSR	1
USA	1
Rye	
USSR	1
Poland	1

For other countries, and other grains, the amounts are smaller. Detailed figures for production, and consumption, of these and other foods can be found, with a bit of effort, in the FAO Year Books in the reference departments of public libraries.

A collage on a large-scale world map could show much more information, say production by the million tons, giving China 104 rice grains and India 6 peanuts, etc.

Note: Copydex and Evostik Impact are good adhesives.

Would you do parts (or all) of this activity with individuals, small groups, or a whole class?

Do you find this the sort of activity which can spread into several subject areas?

How far is the time needed for such activities useful or wasted? Consider it from your own point of view, and from the children's. (See bibliography: 20.)

11 Checking up

Ideas about seeds and seedlings

Everyone, including the teacher and child, comes to science material with some sort of concept already in mind. One intention of science teaching is that early concepts may be extended and improved through selected experiences.

What *concepts* should we expect from a unit of work on seeds and seedlings? The following questions and answers might give a useful outline.

What is a seed?

It comes from a flower.
It is produced in a fruit.
It contains a food store.
It has an embryo plant inside it.
This embryo, given the right conditions, grows first into a seedling.
This seedling, again in the right conditions, develops into a full-grown plant of the same kind as the one which produced the seed.

What factors affect the germination of a seed?

These differ in detail, but depend on whether the plant:

Is still alive.
Is ready to germinate (not still dormant).
Has enough water.
Has enough air.
Has a suitable temperature.

Other factors, such as heredity, internal damage, light, the effect of having been chilled, vernalization, etc, are also important.

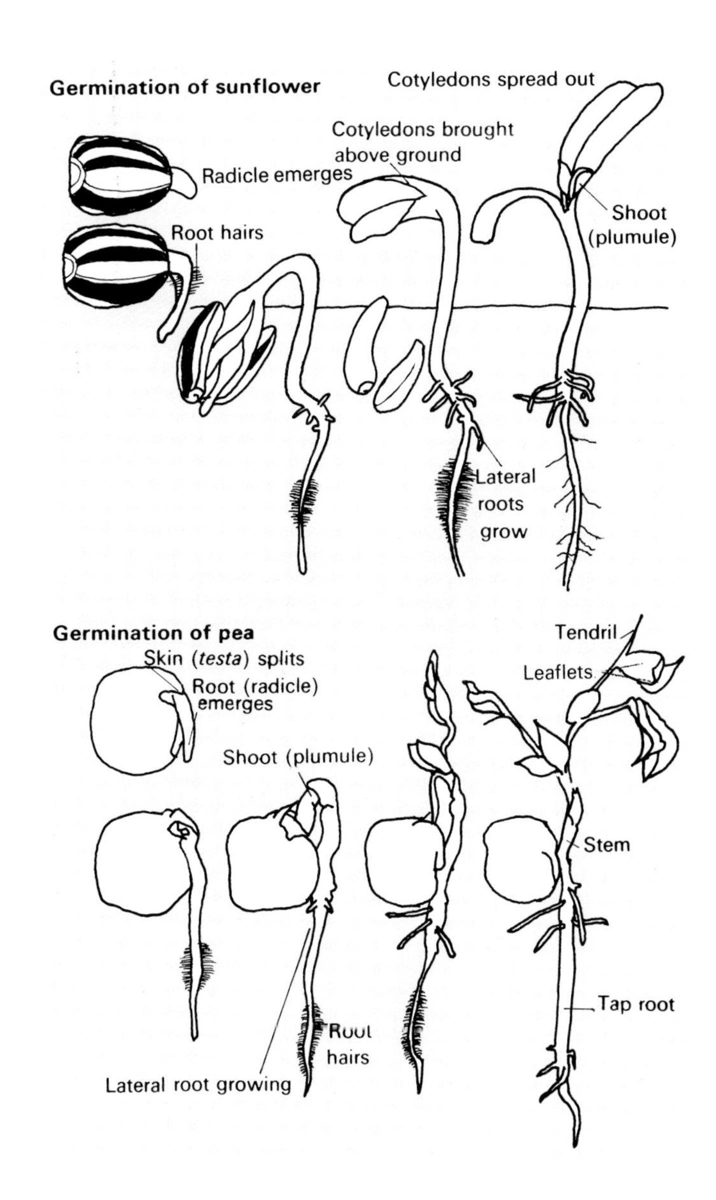

What variables affect a seedling's growth and development towards a full-grown plant?

Internal factors, for example heredity (ie the kind of plant).
Light (amount and direction).
Water.
Temperature.
Air.
Necessary chemicals, in solution and available to the roots.
Support, internal or external.
Freedom from external damage.

What are the stages in a plant's life cycle? How is the generalization about the life cycle important?

Basic experiments

Many experiments with seeds and seedlings under different sets of conditions are described in this book, as well as in others.

Here is a summary of most of the main experiments in which variables are introduced in controlled form.

Experiments and recommended materials

Sorting according to chosen criteria: mustard, cress, beans, peas, sunflower, tree seeds, grains, pips, date stones, coconuts, etc.

Measuring dry seeds (one, two or three dimensions; weight): beans (all kinds), peas, etc.

Soaking Comparing size (one, two or three dimensions) and/or weight of soaked seeds with that of unsoaked seeds: peas and beans.

Germination (or not) under different conditions:

Much/little/no water: mustard or cress.
Dark/light: any seeds; mustard and peas are good.
Warm/cold (refrigerator): any seeds, eg mustard.
Frozen/not frozen seeds: peas. (Note: deep-freeze peas are picked too young.)
Right way up/upside down: beans, maize, sunflowers.
Widely spaced/crowded: mustard or cress.
On different media such as a paper towel, sand, sawdust, Vermiculite if at all possible: mustard, wheat, beans and peas.
Air/no air; water and air/water and almost no air (in a stoppered bottle full of water): mustard or cress.
With/without added nutrients such as Baby Bio.
One-sided light, different light intensities, etc: mustard, peas.

Measuring the time between soaking and sowing, and between germination and reaching a given height, the first leaves, the first flowers, etc: any seeds, especially mustard, cress, peas and beans.

Counting numbers of seeds germinating per number of seeds shown (ie the simple germination rate) : maize, peas, sunflowers. Do not use very small seeds.

New grass seed, last year's grass seed and old grass seed make a good visual comparison without counting.

Measuring the height of the seedling above 'ground' level, and recording : mustard, peas, maize, grass, beans, sunflower, etc.

Measuring the root length (and perhaps counting branch roots) : seedlings wrapped in damp paper roll, eg sunflowers.

Counting numbers of leaves, flowers, seed-pods, seeds, etc : beans, peas.

No child is likely to get through all these activities (for several reasons), though with good planning adults could do so. Would you (a) choose for your pupils, (b) let them choose, (c) organize groups to cover the lot?

Many other activities can be suggested ; they often involve constructing apparatus, collecting materials, or recording information.

Reader self-test

Test yourself with a checklist of important extra points arising from the scientific activities of this book. (Perhaps you knew them anyway.)

1 Which grows faster/first, root or shoot?

2 Why is this an advantage?

3 Which grows faster, a shoot in light or a shoot in the dark?

4 How is this a help to a seed in the soil?

5 How do shoots of beans and peas protect their leaves as they come up through the soil?

6 How are maize, wheat and oat leaves protected as they come up through the soil?

7 What does the existence of *corn*flour suggest as the main food stored in 'corn' (maize)?

8 Which other grains are likely to store the same food substance?

9 What kind of food substance does peanut butter suggest that a peanut stores?

10 How does the colour of seedling leaves grown in the dark compare with that of those grown in light?

11 What does this suggest about the effect of light in a seedling's environment?

12 What advantages may there be to a bean from its tough and almost waterproof seed-skin (*testa*)?

13 What disadvantages may such a tough and almost waterproof seed-skin have for a bean seed?

14 Why do seeds not sprout in the seed packet?

15 In what accidental conditions would they be likely to do so?

16 How many conditions should one change at a time to make sure that an experiment is fair?

17 Why is the soil not as good as damp Vermiculite or blotting paper for a controlled germination experiment?

18 Why can't you continue to use simple damp blotting paper or Vermiculite for a full-grown plant?

19 What is the effect of crowding on the growth of such seedlings as mustard?

20 What comments would you make about the name 'seed potato' for the tuber at the end of an underground stem?

Look for experience of scientific behaviour throughout the activities, for example:

Observing.
Classifying.
Measuring.
Trying out ideas.
Recognizing variables.
Isolating variables.
Making and testing hypotheses.

12 Help with identifying seeds

Pupils, especially boys, often seem only to want or need books which they can use for reference, for finding facts. However, books for primary school pupils dealing with seeds and seedlings tend to give the traditional answers, sometimes even before suggesting the experiments.

Probably the best way to provide a method of identifying seeds, since there is usually a pupil who wants all the names, is to have a shelf of small, clearly labelled jars of the main kinds in use, and a set of

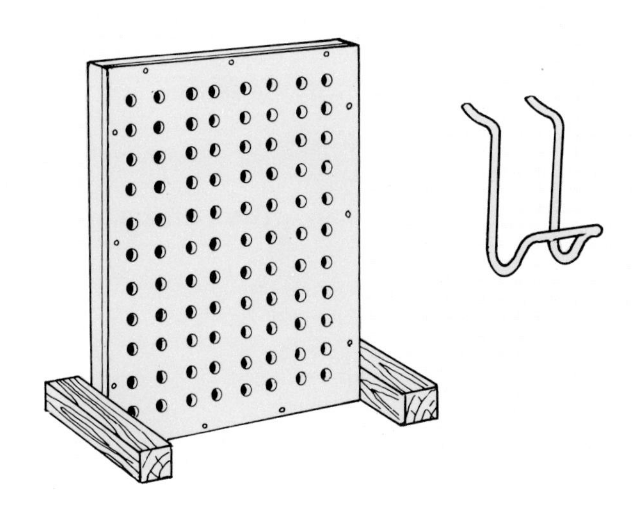

labelled cards with samples. For example, two sycamore fruits, a few onion seeds, maize grains (back and front views) could be stuck onto cards with inch-wide Sellotape. The cards can be made up by the pupils themselves and displayed during the work with seeds and seedlings, perhaps supported on a ledge with a strip of wood glued along the front, or on a sheet of pegboard with poke-through wire display supports.

A picture library is always valuable and should include seed packets mounted on card, and any reasonably reliable pictures such as wheat from All-Bran packets. A standard size and shape for the card mounts should be chosen and a suitable box found for storage. Then the library can be kept for years and added to annually. The box is important, not only for convenience and tidiness, but because loose grains may attract mice.

Farm and Garden Seeds by S. P. Mercer, and other books for agricultural students, are very helpful in naming seeds and in suggesting further lines of experimental work. *Farm and Garden Seeds* gives tables of germination times, suitable temperatures for some crop seeds, average sizes, weights (per thousand) and the number per lb, eg 118 400 onion seeds.

See bibliography: 23.

13 Suggestions for further work

Seeds as human food

1 Grains used as staple foods:

Areas of the world.
Forms of cultivation.
Food values (vitamins, etc).
Food problems (climate).

2 Food products from staple grains: breakfast cereals (rolled oats, cornflakes, shredded wheat, rice crispies), Ryvita.

3 Flour, etc, from staple grains: wheat flour, cornflour, semolina.

4 Flour products: macaroni, spaghetti, noodles.

5 Cooking: bread, pastry, cake mixtures; blancmange.

6 Reaping, harvesting, threshing, milling, grinding corn.

7 Preserving food seeds: canning, freezing, drying.

8 Foods produced from seeds: peanut butter, desiccated coconut, cocoa, coffee (with coffee grinder?).

9 Seeds as flavouring: mustard, pepper (with pepper mill?), caraway seeds (eg in Austrian cabbage or on German rolls).

10 Food tests of the simplest types, such as using *dilute* iodine solution to test for starch, and looking for an oily mark to test for oil (eg in a walnut).

Seeds as animal food

1 Classroom animal foods for gerbils or hamsters. Choices might be maize, wheat, sunflower, peanuts. Note: do not feed oats to hamsters; the sharp husks scratch their cheek-pouch linings.

2 Birdseed for classroom birds, such as budgerigars; a bird-table for wild birds. What do they like, and what do they leave?

3 Sowing and growing birdseed seeds.

4 Oats for ponies, cattle cake, etc.

Seeds for play and in other classroom activities

1 Collages with lentils, linseed, rice, etc.

2 Counting, sorting, number work.

3 Making puppets, dolls' furniture, etc (with horse-chestnuts, for example).

4 Conkers.

5 Threading for (personal?) decoration, eg apple pips, melon pips. Note: pupils may need help in making holes.

6 Seeds, instead of water, in work on *volume.* Rice, for example, flows, and is visible, dry and easy to sweep up.

7 Percussion instruments: 'shakers', maraccas (giving different sound qualities) and coconut-shell halves.

Seeds or seedlings for classroom decoration

1 Dry fruits or seed-heads, eg poppy-heads, pine cones, teazles, wheat, barley, grasses, etc.

2 Small trees grown from seed from oranges, lemons, grapefruit, apples and tomatoes; pine-cone seeds; avocado pear 'stones'; horse-chestnuts, acorns.

Note that these all grow rather slowly, but look decorative.

These very attractive seed collages are being made with old seeds which would probably not germinate well, and with lentils, which could not be expected to grow

14 Workcards: help or hindrance?

College lecture rooms, laboratories and school classrooms are often littered with workcards. What do you think are their special functions, as distinct from those of books, blackboards or the teacher? Or have they none?

Possible special functions of workcards

Perhaps their special function is to organize different children to do different things at the same time? Why? Is it to get all the experiments done by *somebody*? Is it to spread the demand for scarce apparatus? Is it to avoid time-wasting waits for instructions?

Look at a set of published workcards in mathematics or science to find evidence on this organizational function. Do the authors seem to have considered the point?

Teachers often use workcards a great deal, but is this necessarily a measure of their value?

Perhaps workcards are particularly suitable to give more details for each experiment than would be found in a textbook (if any), or would fit onto the blackboard (if any)?

Opposite is an example of a workcard which gives instructions for measuring the size of a seed.

Look at a fairly standard experiment, in a fairly standard textbook, and see how far the instructions would go on a workcard, and if this would be adequate.

What could, or would, you put on a workcard which is probably not in the book?

Ways of measuring the size of a seed.

1. With your partner collect two wooden blocks, a large seed (coconut, avocado 'stone' or horsechestnut) and a ruler marked in centimetres.
2. Put the blocks on a straight line and a little way apart.
3. Put the seed between the blocks so that each end of it touches a block.
4. Put the ruler along your side of the blocks, with the zero (0 cm) end touching the inner corner of the left hand block on your side.
5. Check with this diagram:

6. Measure the length of your seed.
7. Write down your result.
8. Measure another seed in the same way.

Perhaps workcards are most useful to convey ideas and experimental methods by diagrams or sketches, using the 'story without words' technique? Here are two examples.

Keeping your seedlings moist

1 half egg box

2 seeds in damp sawdust

3 sticks (lolly sticks?) through holes

4 plastic bag

Any kind of egg box can be used: the papier-mâché ones soak up more water, but may go mouldy; the transparent plastic ones often have sharp edges

Here we are facing the problem of those children (of any age) who can't really read written instructions; could you try experiments with their minimal literacy? Is it possible to give instructions diagrammatically? If so, would the time taken be justified? Could you perhaps consider making a tape-recording instead, or wouldn't it work? Perhaps you could try a cassette tape-recorder in one corner of the room, with instructions on tape, including frequent instructions such as 'Stop the recorder, now go and do that part, then come back for the next step.' Few classrooms will have a tape-recorder, however, and it might be considered too distracting.

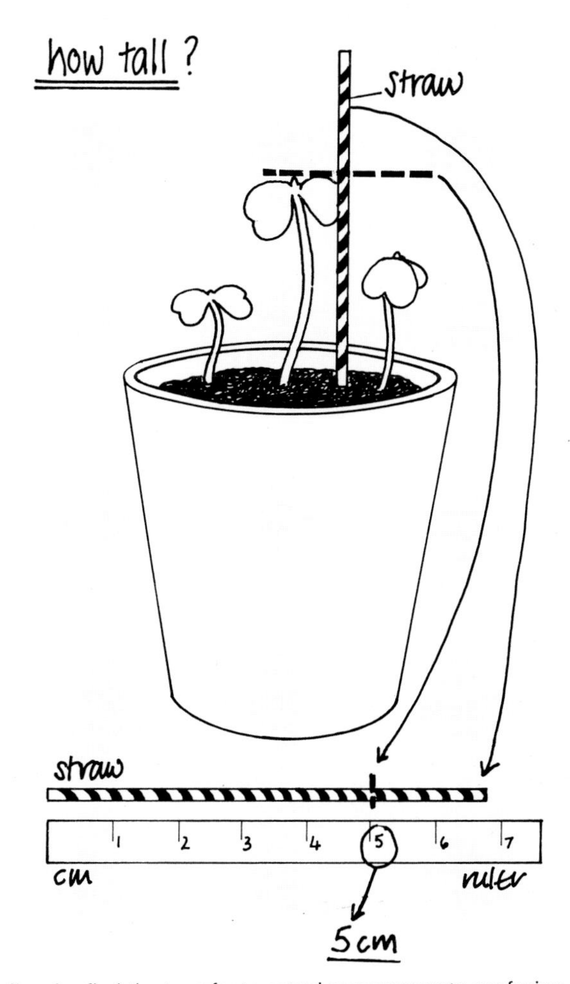

Pupils who find the transfer to actual measurements confusing can cut the actual length of straw with scissors, and stick it bar graph-wise on paper with Sellotape

Try the workcard method with a small group of colleagues, all being constructively critical. First select a set of parallel experiments, such as growing seedlings under different lighting conditions, say in bright light, dim light, red light, strongly one-sided light and darkness.

Each writes a workcard, giving simple instructions for starting each experiment. Then try out someone else's workcard as if you had never heard of the topic before, being 'innocent' without being stupid.

Does it work?

Sorting seeds (and grains?) into groups

1. Suppose you had a walnut, an orange-pip, an acorn, a single peanut, a horse-chestnut and an almond.
2. Make 2 lists – those we eat and those we don't eat.
3. Add 3 more seeds or grains to each list.
4. Now look at the list in point 1 again and make two new lists: those which grow wild in Britain and those which don't. This is more difficult.
5. To each list add three more you are sure about.
6. Consider the seeds in point 1 again. Think out and use another way of sorting them into 2 different groups.

This workcard might be used by abler pupils as a starting point for thinking exercises and simple book research

Sorting seeds into groups

1. Collect a small pot of mixed seeds [about five different kinds would do] and six small dishes [perhaps 8oz margarine tubs].
2. Spread out some of your mixed seeds in front of you and see what different kinds of seed you have there.
3. Sort the mixture quickly into dishes, one kind in each, until they are all sorted.
4. Count the number of seeds in each dish.
5. Write down what makes each kind of seed different from the others (colour, size, etc). Then note how many you have of each kind.
6. Draw one of each kind.

This kind of workcard includes easy practical exercises (points 1–4, 6) and one more difficult problem

Workcards can be very useful with older or more able pupils, to extend their thinking and writing. Two examples are given above. In the one on the right with the square brackets, the details are added by the teacher.

What about the actual cost of the card, of the plastic coating, etc, and of your time? How long would it take you to make a set for the whole class? Perhaps you can use a form of duplicating to produce small numbers of copies, but most duplicators do not take kindly to card.

Try as many varieties of your own workcard as you can (large, small, disposable work-sheet type, etc), and find out how they work. Make your own analysis of cost and effectiveness; compare with any printed workcards you can find in use (eg maths cards).

Bibliography

For children to use

1 Fice, R. H. C. and Simkiss, I. M. (1973) *We Discover: Plants*. E. J. Arnold. (This is for top infants.)
2 Griffin-King, J. (1969) *Indoor Gardening*. Ladybird. Wills and Hepworth. (This is for all ages.)
3 McTrusty, R. (1974) *Dandelion Year*. A. & C. Black. (This is for infant non-readers.)
4 Newing, F. E. and Bowood, R. (1965) *Plants and How They Grow*. Ladybird Natural History Series. Wills and Hepworth.
5 Starters: Activities (1972) *Growing things indoors.* Macdonald Educational. (This is for infant early readers.)

For direct work with children

6 Bainbridge, J. W., Stockdale, R. W. and Wastnedge, E. R. (1970) *Junior Science Source Book*. Collins. See pages 102-103, 106, 112-113, 115.
7 Bishop, O. N. (1971) *Outdoor Biology, Volume 1*. John Murray. See pages 30, 36, 39.
8 Carin, A. A. and Sund, R. B. (1970) *Teaching Science Through Discovery*. 2nd edition. Charles E. Merrill.
9 Elementary Science Study (1967) *Teacher's Guide: Growing Seeds*. McGraw-Hill.
10 Elementary Science Study (1967) *Teacher's Guide: The Life of Beans and Peas*. McGraw-Hill.
11 Finch, I. (1971) *Nature Study and Science*. Longman. See sections 28/1, 32/1-17, 33/1-4, 34/1-6, 35/1-4, 36/1-10d, 45/2.
12 Nuffield Combined Science (1970) *Activities Pack 2, Book 8*. Longman. See pages 8, 10.
13 Nuffield Junior Science (1967) *Animals and Plants*. Collins. See pages 236-244.
14 Nuffield Mathematics Project (1967) *Mathematics Begins*. Chambers. This deals with sorting at infant level.
15 Nuffield/CEDO Handbook (1970) *Mathematics—The First Three Years*. Chambers/John Murray. This deals with graphic methods of recording and communicating.
16 School Natural Science Society (1967) *Nature Activities in Schools: Nature Study with Children Under 8 and Concrete Yard Gardening*. Leaflet No. 13. School Natural Science Society.
17 Schools Council Science 5/13 (1972) *Early experiences*. Macdonald Educational.
18 Thier, H. D. (1971) *Teaching Elementary Science: A Laboratory Approach*. D. C. Heath.

For further information and ideas

19 Claridge, D. W. 'Biology notes', *School Science Review* 186. Association for Science Education/John Murray. See pages 78-81 on seed dispersal.
20 Jackson, N. and Penn, P. (1969) *A Dictionary of Natural Resources and their Principal Uses*. 2nd edition. Pergamon.
21 Mackean, D. G. (1971) *Experimental Work in Biology. Volume 5: Germination and Tropisms*. John Murray. See pages 6-9, 22-24, etc.
22 Mackean, D. G. (1970) *Introduction to Biology*. John Murray.
23 Mercer, S. P. (1948) *Farm and Garden Seeds*. Crosby Lockwood.
24 Revised Nuffield Biology (1975) *Teachers' guide 4*. Longman. See page 102 for information about mini-greenhouses. If you do not have the Revised Nuffield Biology books, consult page 62 of the following book:
25 Nuffield Biology (1966) *Teachers' Guide V*.

26 Prime, C. T. (1971) *Experiments for Young Botanists*. G. Bell. See pages 26-30, 35-69.
27 Sands, M. K. (1971) *Problems in Plant Physiology*. John Murray. See pages 18-28.
28 Tampion J. (December 1971) 'Unusual monocotyledonous seed for germination studies', *School Science Review* **183**. Association for Science Education/ John Murray. See pages 336-339 on date seedlings.

Filmstrip

'Life cycles of flowering plants', Common Ground/ Longman. 44 frames and notes. ISBN 0 7056 2021 2.